NOTARY PUBLIC JOURNAL

LARGE ENTRIES

All rights reserved. No part of this publication may be
reproduced, stored in a retrieval system, or transmitted in any form or by any means, electronic, mechanical, photocopying or otherwise, without
the prior permission of the copyright owner.

This book provides for the recording of 250 large sized entries. It
conveniently organizes the categories to be recorded and includes a "Notes" area for additional information.

Notaries Public ... hold an office which can trace its origins back to
ancient Rome when they were called scribae, tabellius or notarius.
They are easily the oldest continuing branch of the
legal profession worldwide.

© Copyright 2018 by Snowball Publishing

www.snowballpublishing.com

info@snowballpublishing.com

For information regarding special discounts for bulk purchases, please contact **Snowball Publishing** at

sale@snowballpublishing.com

NOTARY PUBLIC JOURNAL – LARGE ENTRIES | 3

1 | Service: ☐ Acknowledgment ☐ Oath/Affirmation ☐ Jurat ☐ Other/See Notes Fee $_____ Travel_____

Name (print)	Document type /Doc. name	Witness Name (print)	Date and Time Notarized _____ ___ _____ am / pm
Phone # / E-mail	Date of document	Witness Phone # / E-mail	Print of Right Thumb
Address	Satisfactory evidence of ID ☐ Driver's license ☐ Known Personally ☐ Credible Witness(es) ☐ Passport ☐ I.D. Card ☐ See Notes	Witness Address	
☐ ID. Issued by ☐ I.D. Number	☐ Expiration Date ☐ Issue Date	Notes	
Signer Signature		Witness Signature	

2 | Service: ☐ Acknowledgment ☐ Oath/Affirmation ☐ Jurat ☐ Other/See Notes Fee $_____ Travel_____

Name (print)	Document type /Doc. name	Witness Name (print)	Date and Time Notarized _____ ___ _____ am / pm
Phone # / E-mail	Date of document	Witness Phone # / E-mail	Print of Right Thumb
Address	Satisfactory evidence of ID ☐ Driver's license ☐ Known Personally ☐ Credible Witness(es) ☐ Passport ☐ I.D. Card ☐ See Notes	Witness Address	
☐ ID. Issued by ☐ I.D. Number	☐ Expiration Date ☐ Issue Date	Notes	
Signer Signature		Witness Signature	

NOTARY PUBLIC JOURNAL – LARGE ENTRIES

3 | Service: ☐ Acknowledgment ☐ Oath/Affirmation ☐ Jurat ☐ Other/See Notes   Fee $_____   Travel_____

Name (print)	Document type /Doc. name	Witness Name (print)	Date and Time Notarized _____ ____ _____ am / pm
Phone # / E-mail	Date of document	Witness Phone # / E-mail	Print of Right Thumb
Address	Satisfactory evidence of ID ☐ Driver's license ☐ Known Personally ☐ Credible Witness(es) ☐ Passport ☐ I.D. Card ☐ See Notes	Witness Address	
☐ ID. Issued by ☐ I.D. Number	☐ Expiration Date ☐ Issue Date	Notes	
Signer Signature		Witness Signature	

4 | Service: ☐ Acknowledgment ☐ Oath/Affirmation ☐ Jurat ☐ Other/See Notes   Fee $_____   Travel_____

Name (print)	Document type /Doc. name	Witness Name (print)	Date and Time Notarized _____ ____ _____ am / pm
Phone # / E-mail	Date of document	Witness Phone # / E-mail	Print of Right Thumb
Address	Satisfactory evidence of ID ☐ Driver's license ☐ Known Personally ☐ Credible Witness(es) ☐ Passport ☐ I.D. Card ☐ See Notes	Witness Address	
☐ ID. Issued by ☐ I.D. Number	☐ Expiration Date ☐ Issue Date	Notes	
Signer Signature		Witness Signature	

NOTARY PUBLIC JOURNAL – LARGE ENTRIES | 5

5 | Service: ☐ Acknowledgment ☐ Oath/Affirmation ☐ Jurat ☐ Other/See Notes   Fee $_____   Travel_____

Name (print)	Document type /Doc. name	Witness Name (print)	Date and Time Notarized _____ ___ _____ am / pm
Phone # / E-mail	Date of document	Witness Phone # / E-mail	Print of Right Thumb
Address	Satisfactory evidence of ID ☐ Driver's license ☐ Known Personally ☐ Credible Witness(es) ☐ Passport ☐ I.D. Card ☐ See Notes	Witness Address	
☐ ID. Issued by ☐ I.D. Number	☐ Expiration Date ☐ Issue Date	Notes	
Signer Signature		Witness Signature	

6 | Service: ☐ Acknowledgment ☐ Oath/Affirmation ☐ Jurat ☐ Other/See Notes   Fee $_____   Travel_____

Name (print)	Document type /Doc. name	Witness Name (print)	Date and Time Notarized _____ ___ _____ am / pm
Phone # / E-mail	Date of document	Witness Phone # / E-mail	Print of Right Thumb
Address	Satisfactory evidence of ID ☐ Driver's license ☐ Known Personally ☐ Credible Witness(es) ☐ Passport ☐ I.D. Card ☐ See Notes	Witness Address	
☐ ID. Issued by ☐ I.D. Number	☐ Expiration Date ☐ Issue Date	Notes	
Signer Signature		Witness Signature	

6 | NOTARY PUBLIC JOURNAL – LARGE ENTRIES

7 — Service: ☐ Acknowledgment ☐ Oath/Affirmation ☐ Jurat ☐ Other/See Notes   Fee $_____   Travel_____

Name (print)	Document type /Doc. name	Witness Name (print)	Date and Time Notarized _____ ___ ___ am / pm
Phone # / E-mail	Date of document	Witness Phone # / E-mail	Print of Right Thumb
Address	Satisfactory evidence of ID ☐ Driver's license ☐ Known Personally ☐ Credible Witness(es) ☐ Passport ☐ I.D. Card ☐ See Notes	Witness Address	
☐ ID. Issued by ☐ I.D. Number	☐ Expiration Date ☐ Issue Date	Notes	
Signer Signature		Witness Signature	

8 — Service: ☐ Acknowledgment ☐ Oath/Affirmation ☐ Jurat ☐ Other/See Notes   Fee $_____   Travel_____

Name (print)	Document type /Doc. name	Witness Name (print)	Date and Time Notarized _____ ___ ___ am / pm
Phone # / E-mail	Date of document	Witness Phone # / E-mail	Print of Right Thumb
Address	Satisfactory evidence of ID ☐ Driver's license ☐ Known Personally ☐ Credible Witness(es) ☐ Passport ☐ I.D. Card ☐ See Notes	Witness Address	
☐ ID. Issued by ☐ I.D. Number	☐ Expiration Date ☐ Issue Date	Notes	
Signer Signature		Witness Signature	

NOTARY PUBLIC JOURNAL – LARGE ENTRIES | 7

9 | Service: ☐ Acknowledgment ☐ Oath/Affirmation ☐ Jurat ☐ Other/See Notes   Fee $_____   Travel_____

Name (print)	Document type /Doc. name	Witness Name (print)	Date and Time Notarized _____ ___ _____ am / pm
Phone # / E-mail	Date of document	Witness Phone # / E-mail	Print of Right Thumb
Address	Satisfactory evidence of ID ☐ Driver's license ☐ Known Personally ☐ Credible Witness(es) ☐ Passport ☐ I.D. Card ☐ See Notes	Witness Address	
☐ ID. Issued by ☐ I.D. Number	☐ Expiration Date ☐ Issue Date	Notes	
Signer Signature		Witness Signature	

10 | Service: ☐ Acknowledgment ☐ Oath/Affirmation ☐ Jurat ☐ Other/See Notes   Fee $_____   Travel_____

Name (print)	Document type /Doc. name	Witness Name (print)	Date and Time Notarized _____ ___ _____ am / pm
Phone # / E-mail	Date of document	Witness Phone # / E-mail	Print of Right Thumb
Address	Satisfactory evidence of ID ☐ Driver's license ☐ Known Personally ☐ Credible Witness(es) ☐ Passport ☐ I.D. Card ☐ See Notes	Witness Address	
☐ ID. Issued by ☐ I.D. Number	☐ Expiration Date ☐ Issue Date	Notes	
Signer Signature		Witness Signature	

NOTARY PUBLIC JOURNAL – LARGE ENTRIES

11 — Service: ☐ Acknowledgment ☐ Oath/Affirmation ☐ Jurat ☐ Other/See Notes Fee $_____ Travel_____

Name (print)	Document type /Doc. name	Witness Name (print)	Date and Time Notarized _____ ___ ___ am / pm
Phone # / E-mail	Date of document	Witness Phone # / E-mail	Print of Right Thumb
Address	Satisfactory evidence of ID ☐ Driver's license ☐ Known Personally ☐ Credible Witness(es) ☐ Passport ☐ I.D. Card ☐ See Notes	Witness Address	
☐ ID. Issued by ☐ I.D. Number	☐ Expiration Date ☐ Issue Date	Notes	
Signer Signature		Witness Signature	

12 — Service: ☐ Acknowledgment ☐ Oath/Affirmation ☐ Jurat ☐ Other/See Notes Fee $_____ Travel_____

Name (print)	Document type /Doc. name	Witness Name (print)	Date and Time Notarized _____ ___ ___ am / pm
Phone # / E-mail	Date of document	Witness Phone # / E-mail	Print of Right Thumb
Address	Satisfactory evidence of ID ☐ Driver's license ☐ Known Personally ☐ Credible Witness(es) ☐ Passport ☐ I.D. Card ☐ See Notes	Witness Address	
☐ ID. Issued by ☐ I.D. Number	☐ Expiration Date ☐ Issue Date	Notes	
Signer Signature		Witness Signature	

13

Service: ☐ Acknowledgment ☐ Oath/Affirmation ☐ Jurat ☐ Other/See Notes   Fee $_____   Travel_____

Name (print)	Document type /Doc. name	Witness Name (print)	Date and Time Notarized _____ ___ _____ am / pm
Phone # / E-mail	Date of document	Witness Phone # / E-mail	Print of Right Thumb
Address	Satisfactory evidence of ID ☐ Driver's license ☐ Known Personally ☐ Credible Witness(es) ☐ Passport ☐ I.D. Card ☐ See Notes	Witness Address	
☐ ID. Issued by ☐ I.D. Number	☐ Expiration Date ☐ Issue Date	Notes	
Signer Signature		Witness Signature	

14

Service: ☐ Acknowledgment ☐ Oath/Affirmation ☐ Jurat ☐ Other/See Notes   Fee $_____   Travel_____

Name (print)	Document type /Doc. name	Witness Name (print)	Date and Time Notarized _____ ___ _____ am / pm
Phone # / E-mail	Date of document	Witness Phone # / E-mail	Print of Right Thumb
Address	Satisfactory evidence of ID ☐ Driver's license ☐ Known Personally ☐ Credible Witness(es) ☐ Passport ☐ I.D. Card ☐ See Notes	Witness Address	
☐ ID. Issued by ☐ I.D. Number	☐ Expiration Date ☐ Issue Date	Notes	
Signer Signature		Witness Signature	

NOTARY PUBLIC JOURNAL – LARGE ENTRIES

15 — Service: ☐ Acknowledgment ☐ Oath/Affirmation ☐ Jurat ☐ Other/See Notes   Fee $_____   Travel_____

Name (print)	Document type /Doc. name	Witness Name (print)	Date and Time Notarized _____ ___ _____ am / pm
Phone # / E-mail	Date of document	Witness Phone # / E-mail	Print of Right Thumb
Address	Satisfactory evidence of ID ☐ Driver's license ☐ Known Personally ☐ Credible Witness(es) ☐ Passport ☐ I.D. Card ☐ See Notes	Witness Address	
☐ ID. Issued by	☐ Expiration Date	Notes	
☐ I.D. Number	☐ Issue Date		
Signer Signature		Witness Signature	

16 — Service: ☐ Acknowledgment ☐ Oath/Affirmation ☐ Jurat ☐ Other/See Notes   Fee $_____   Travel_____

Name (print)	Document type /Doc. name	Witness Name (print)	Date and Time Notarized _____ ___ _____ am / pm
Phone # / E-mail	Date of document	Witness Phone # / E-mail	Print of Right Thumb
Address	Satisfactory evidence of ID ☐ Driver's license ☐ Known Personally ☐ Credible Witness(es) ☐ Passport ☐ I.D. Card ☐ See Notes	Witness Address	
☐ ID. Issued by	☐ Expiration Date	Notes	
☐ I.D. Number	☐ Issue Date		
Signer Signature		Witness Signature	

NOTARY PUBLIC JOURNAL – LARGE ENTRIES | 11

17 | Service: ☐ Acknowledgment ☐ Oath/Affirmation ☐ Jurat ☐ Other/See Notes Fee $_____ Travel_____

Name (print)	Document type /Doc. name	Witness Name (print)	Date and Time Notarized _____ ___ _____ am / pm
Phone # / E-mail	Date of document	Witness Phone # / E-mail	Print of Right Thumb
Address	Satisfactory evidence of ID ☐ Driver's license ☐ Known Personally ☐ Credible Witness(es) ☐ Passport ☐ I.D. Card ☐ See Notes	Witness Address	
☐ ID. Issued by ☐ I.D. Number	☐ Expiration Date ☐ Issue Date	Notes	
Signer Signature		Witness Signature	

18 | Service: ☐ Acknowledgment ☐ Oath/Affirmation ☐ Jurat ☐ Other/See Notes Fee $_____ Travel_____

Name (print)	Document type /Doc. name	Witness Name (print)	Date and Time Notarized _____ ___ _____ am / pm
Phone # / E-mail	Date of document	Witness Phone # / E-mail	Print of Right Thumb
Address	Satisfactory evidence of ID ☐ Driver's license ☐ Known Personally ☐ Credible Witness(es) ☐ Passport ☐ I.D. Card ☐ See Notes	Witness Address	
☐ ID. Issued by ☐ I.D. Number	☐ Expiration Date ☐ Issue Date	Notes	
Signer Signature		Witness Signature	

NOTARY PUBLIC JOURNAL – LARGE ENTRIES

19
Service: ☐ Acknowledgment ☐ Oath/Affirmation ☐ Jurat ☐ Other/See Notes Fee $_____ Travel_____

Name (print)	Document type /Doc. name	Witness Name (print)	Date and Time Notarized _____ ___ ___ am / pm
Phone # / E-mail	Date of document	Witness Phone # / E-mail	Print of Right Thumb
Address	Satisfactory evidence of ID ☐ Driver's license ☐ Known Personally ☐ Credible Witness(es) ☐ Passport ☐ I.D. Card ☐ See Notes	Witness Address	
☐ ID. Issued by ☐ I.D. Number	☐ Expiration Date ☐ Issue Date	Notes	
Signer Signature		Witness Signature	

20
Service: ☐ Acknowledgment ☐ Oath/Affirmation ☐ Jurat ☐ Other/See Notes Fee $_____ Travel_____

Name (print)	Document type /Doc. name	Witness Name (print)	Date and Time Notarized _____ ___ ___ am / pm
Phone # / E-mail	Date of document	Witness Phone # / E-mail	Print of Right Thumb
Address	Satisfactory evidence of ID ☐ Driver's license ☐ Known Personally ☐ Credible Witness(es) ☐ Passport ☐ I.D. Card ☐ See Notes	Witness Address	
☐ ID. Issued by ☐ I.D. Number	☐ Expiration Date ☐ Issue Date	Notes	
Signer Signature		Witness Signature	

NOTARY PUBLIC JOURNAL – LARGE ENTRIES | 13

21
Service: ☐ Acknowledgment ☐ Oath/Affirmation ☐ Jurat ☐ Other/See Notes   Fee $_____   Travel_____

Name (print)	Document type /Doc. name	Witness Name (print)	Date and Time Notarized _____ ___ _____ am / pm
Phone # / E-mail	Date of document	Witness Phone # / E-mail	Print of Right Thumb
Address	Satisfactory evidence of ID ☐ Driver's license ☐ Known Personally ☐ Credible Witness(es) ☐ Passport ☐ I.D. Card ☐ See Notes	Witness Address	
☐ ID. Issued by ☐ I.D. Number	☐ Expiration Date ☐ Issue Date	Notes	
Signer Signature		Witness Signature	

22
Service: ☐ Acknowledgment ☐ Oath/Affirmation ☐ Jurat ☐ Other/See Notes   Fee $_____   Travel_____

Name (print)	Document type /Doc. name	Witness Name (print)	Date and Time Notarized _____ ___ _____ am / pm
Phone # / E-mail	Date of document	Witness Phone # / E-mail	Print of Right Thumb
Address	Satisfactory evidence of ID ☐ Driver's license ☐ Known Personally ☐ Credible Witness(es) ☐ Passport ☐ I.D. Card ☐ See Notes	Witness Address	
☐ ID. Issued by ☐ I.D. Number	☐ Expiration Date ☐ Issue Date	Notes	
Signer Signature		Witness Signature	

14 | NOTARY PUBLIC JOURNAL – LARGE ENTRIES

23 Service: ☐ Acknowledgment ☐ Oath/Affirmation ☐ Jurat ☐ Other/See Notes Fee $_____ Travel_____

Name (print)	Document type /Doc. name	Witness Name (print)	Date and Time Notarized _____ ___ ___ am / pm
Phone # / E-mail	Date of document	Witness Phone # / E-mail	Print of Right Thumb
Address	Satisfactory evidence of ID ☐ Driver's license ☐ Known Personally ☐ Credible Witness(es) ☐ Passport ☐ I.D. Card ☐ See Notes	Witness Address	
☐ ID. Issued by ☐ I.D. Number	☐ Expiration Date ☐ Issue Date	Notes	
Signer Signature		Witness Signature	

24 Service: ☐ Acknowledgment ☐ Oath/Affirmation ☐ Jurat ☐ Other/See Notes Fee $_____ Travel_____

Name (print)	Document type /Doc. name	Witness Name (print)	Date and Time Notarized _____ ___ ___ am / pm
Phone # / E-mail	Date of document	Witness Phone # / E-mail	Print of Right Thumb
Address	Satisfactory evidence of ID ☐ Driver's license ☐ Known Personally ☐ Credible Witness(es) ☐ Passport ☐ I.D. Card ☐ See Notes	Witness Address	
☐ ID. Issued by ☐ I.D. Number	☐ Expiration Date ☐ Issue Date	Notes	
Signer Signature		Witness Signature	

NOTARY PUBLIC JOURNAL – LARGE ENTRIES | 15

25
Service: ☐ Acknowledgment ☐ Oath/Affirmation ☐ Jurat ☐ Other/See Notes Fee $_____ Travel_____

Name (print)	Document type /Doc. name	Witness Name (print)	Date and Time Notarized _____ ___ _____ am / pm
Phone # / E-mail	Date of document	Witness Phone # / E-mail	Print of Right Thumb
Address	Satisfactory evidence of ID ☐ Driver's license ☐ Known Personally ☐ Credible Witness(es) ☐ Passport ☐ I.D. Card ☐ See Notes	Witness Address	
☐ ID. Issued by ☐ I.D. Number	☐ Expiration Date ☐ Issue Date	Notes	
Signer Signature		Witness Signature	

26
Service: ☐ Acknowledgment ☐ Oath/Affirmation ☐ Jurat ☐ Other/See Notes Fee $_____ Travel_____

Name (print)	Document type /Doc. name	Witness Name (print)	Date and Time Notarized _____ ___ _____ am / pm
Phone # / E-mail	Date of document	Witness Phone # / E-mail	Print of Right Thumb
Address	Satisfactory evidence of ID ☐ Driver's license ☐ Known Personally ☐ Credible Witness(es) ☐ Passport ☐ I.D. Card ☐ See Notes	Witness Address	
☐ ID. Issued by ☐ I.D. Number	☐ Expiration Date ☐ Issue Date	Notes	
Signer Signature		Witness Signature	

16 | NOTARY PUBLIC JOURNAL – LARGE ENTRIES

27 — Service: ☐ Acknowledgment ☐ Oath/Affirmation ☐ Jurat ☐ Other/See Notes   Fee $_____   Travel_____

Name (print)	Document type /Doc. name	Witness Name (print)	Date and Time Notarized
			_____ ____ _____ am / pm
Phone # / E-mail	Date of document	Witness Phone # / E-mail	Print of Right Thumb
Address	Satisfactory evidence of ID ☐ Driver's license ☐ Known Personally ☐ Credible Witness(es) ☐ Passport ☐ I.D. Card ☐ See Notes	Witness Address	
☐ ID. Issued by	☐ Expiration Date	Notes	
☐ I.D. Number	☐ Issue Date		
Signer Signature		Witness Signature	

28 — Service: ☐ Acknowledgment ☐ Oath/Affirmation ☐ Jurat ☐ Other/See Notes   Fee $_____   Travel_____

Name (print)	Document type /Doc. name	Witness Name (print)	Date and Time Notarized
			_____ ____ _____ am / pm
Phone # / E-mail	Date of document	Witness Phone # / E-mail	Print of Right Thumb
Address	Satisfactory evidence of ID ☐ Driver's license ☐ Known Personally ☐ Credible Witness(es) ☐ Passport ☐ I.D. Card ☐ See Notes	Witness Address	
☐ ID. Issued by	☐ Expiration Date	Notes	
☐ I.D. Number	☐ Issue Date		
Signer Signature		Witness Signature	

NOTARY PUBLIC JOURNAL – LARGE ENTRIES | 17

29 Service: ☐ Acknowledgment ☐ Oath/Affirmation ☐ Jurat ☐ Other/See Notes Fee $_____ Travel_____

Name (print)	Document type /Doc. name	Witness Name (print)	Date and Time Notarized _____ ___ ___ am / pm
Phone # / E-mail	Date of document	Witness Phone # / E-mail	Print of Right Thumb
Address	Satisfactory evidence of ID ☐ Driver's license ☐ Known Personally ☐ Credible Witness(es) ☐ Passport ☐ I.D. Card ☐ See Notes	Witness Address	
☐ ID. Issued by ☐ I.D. Number	☐ Expiration Date ☐ Issue Date	Notes	
Signer Signature		Witness Signature	

30 Service: ☐ Acknowledgment ☐ Oath/Affirmation ☐ Jurat ☐ Other/See Notes Fee $_____ Travel_____

Name (print)	Document type /Doc. name	Witness Name (print)	Date and Time Notarized _____ ___ ___ am / pm
Phone # / E-mail	Date of document	Witness Phone # / E-mail	Print of Right Thumb
Address	Satisfactory evidence of ID ☐ Driver's license ☐ Known Personally ☐ Credible Witness(es) ☐ Passport ☐ I.D. Card ☐ See Notes	Witness Address	
☐ ID. Issued by ☐ I.D. Number	☐ Expiration Date ☐ Issue Date	Notes	
Signer Signature		Witness Signature	

18 | NOTARY PUBLIC JOURNAL – LARGE ENTRIES

31 | Service: ☐ Acknowledgment ☐ Oath/Affirmation ☐ Jurat ☐ Other/See Notes   Fee $_____   Travel_____

Name (print)	Document type /Doc. name	Witness Name (print)	Date and Time Notarized _____ ___ ___ am / pm
Phone # / E-mail	Date of document	Witness Phone # / E-mail	Print of Right Thumb
Address	Satisfactory evidence of ID ☐ Driver's license ☐ Known Personally ☐ Credible Witness(es) ☐ Passport ☐ I.D. Card ☐ See Notes	Witness Address	
☐ ID. Issued by ☐ I.D. Number	☐ Expiration Date ☐ Issue Date	Notes	
Signer Signature		Witness Signature	

32 | Service: ☐ Acknowledgment ☐ Oath/Affirmation ☐ Jurat ☐ Other/See Notes   Fee $_____   Travel_____

Name (print)	Document type /Doc. name	Witness Name (print)	Date and Time Notarized _____ ___ ___ am / pm
Phone # / E-mail	Date of document	Witness Phone # / E-mail	Print of Right Thumb
Address	Satisfactory evidence of ID ☐ Driver's license ☐ Known Personally ☐ Credible Witness(es) ☐ Passport ☐ I.D. Card ☐ See Notes	Witness Address	
☐ ID. Issued by ☐ I.D. Number	☐ Expiration Date ☐ Issue Date	Notes	
Signer Signature		Witness Signature	

NOTARY PUBLIC JOURNAL – LARGE ENTRIES | 19

33 | Service: ☐ Acknowledgment ☐ Oath/Affirmation ☐ Jurat ☐ Other/See Notes Fee $_____ Travel_____

Name (print)	Document type /Doc. name	Witness Name (print)	Date and Time Notarized _____ ___ _____ am / pm
Phone # / E-mail	Date of document	Witness Phone # / E-mail	Print of Right Thumb
Address	Satisfactory evidence of ID ☐ Driver's license ☐ Known Personally ☐ Credible Witness(es) ☐ Passport ☐ I.D. Card ☐ See Notes	Witness Address	
☐ ID. Issued by ☐ I.D. Number	☐ Expiration Date ☐ Issue Date	Notes	
Signer Signature		Witness Signature	

34 | Service: ☐ Acknowledgment ☐ Oath/Affirmation ☐ Jurat ☐ Other/See Notes Fee $_____ Travel_____

Name (print)	Document type /Doc. name	Witness Name (print)	Date and Time Notarized _____ ___ _____ am / pm
Phone # / E-mail	Date of document	Witness Phone # / E-mail	Print of Right Thumb
Address	Satisfactory evidence of ID ☐ Driver's license ☐ Known Personally ☐ Credible Witness(es) ☐ Passport ☐ I.D. Card ☐ See Notes	Witness Address	
☐ ID. Issued by ☐ I.D. Number	☐ Expiration Date ☐ Issue Date	Notes	
Signer Signature		Witness Signature	

NOTARY PUBLIC JOURNAL – LARGE ENTRIES

35 Service: ☐ Acknowledgment ☐ Oath/Affirmation ☐ Jurat ☐ Other/See Notes   Fee $_____   Travel_____

Name (print)	Document type /Doc. name	Witness Name (print)	Date and Time Notarized _____ ____ ____ am / pm
Phone # / E-mail	Date of document	Witness Phone # / E-mail	Print of Right Thumb
Address	Satisfactory evidence of ID ☐ Driver's license ☐ Known Personally ☐ Credible Witness(es) ☐ Passport ☐ I.D. Card ☐ See Notes	Witness Address	
☐ ID. Issued by ☐ I.D. Number	☐ Expiration Date ☐ Issue Date	Notes	
Signer Signature		Witness Signature	

36 Service: ☐ Acknowledgment ☐ Oath/Affirmation ☐ Jurat ☐ Other/See Notes   Fee $_____   Travel_____

Name (print)	Document type /Doc. name	Witness Name (print)	Date and Time Notarized _____ ____ ____ am / pm
Phone # / E-mail	Date of document	Witness Phone # / E-mail	Print of Right Thumb
Address	Satisfactory evidence of ID ☐ Driver's license ☐ Known Personally ☐ Credible Witness(es) ☐ Passport ☐ I.D. Card ☐ See Notes	Witness Address	
☐ ID. Issued by ☐ I.D. Number	☐ Expiration Date ☐ Issue Date	Notes	
Signer Signature		Witness Signature	

37

Service: ☐ Acknowledgment ☐ Oath/Affirmation ☐ Jurat ☐ Other/See Notes Fee $_____ Travel_____

Name (print)	Document type /Doc. name	Witness Name (print)	Date and Time Notarized _____ ___ _____ am / pm
Phone # / E-mail	Date of document	Witness Phone # / E-mail	Print of Right Thumb
Address	Satisfactory evidence of ID ☐ Driver's license ☐ Known Personally ☐ Credible Witness(es) ☐ Passport ☐ I.D. Card ☐ See Notes	Witness Address	
☐ ID. Issued by ☐ I.D. Number	☐ Expiration Date ☐ Issue Date	Notes	
Signer Signature		Witness Signature	

38

Service: ☐ Acknowledgment ☐ Oath/Affirmation ☐ Jurat ☐ Other/See Notes Fee $_____ Travel_____

Name (print)	Document type /Doc. name	Witness Name (print)	Date and Time Notarized _____ ___ _____ am / pm
Phone # / E-mail	Date of document	Witness Phone # / E-mail	Print of Right Thumb
Address	Satisfactory evidence of ID ☐ Driver's license ☐ Known Personally ☐ Credible Witness(es) ☐ Passport ☐ I.D. Card ☐ See Notes	Witness Address	
☐ ID. Issued by ☐ I.D. Number	☐ Expiration Date ☐ Issue Date	Notes	
Signer Signature		Witness Signature	

NOTARY PUBLIC JOURNAL – LARGE ENTRIES

39 Service: ☐ Acknowledgment ☐ Oath/Affirmation ☐ Jurat ☐ Other/See Notes Fee $_____ Travel_____

Name (print)	Document type /Doc. name	Witness Name (print)	Date and Time Notarized _____ ___ _____ am / pm
Phone # / E-mail	Date of document	Witness Phone # / E-mail	Print of Right Thumb
Address	Satisfactory evidence of ID ☐ Driver's license ☐ Known Personally ☐ Credible Witness(es) ☐ Passport ☐ I.D. Card ☐ See Notes	Witness Address	
☐ ID. Issued by ☐ I.D. Number	☐ Expiration Date ☐ Issue Date	Notes	
Signer Signature		Witness Signature	

40 Service: ☐ Acknowledgment ☐ Oath/Affirmation ☐ Jurat ☐ Other/See Notes Fee $_____ Travel_____

Name (print)	Document type /Doc. name	Witness Name (print)	Date and Time Notarized _____ ___ _____ am / pm
Phone # / E-mail	Date of document	Witness Phone # / E-mail	Print of Right Thumb
Address	Satisfactory evidence of ID ☐ Driver's license ☐ Known Personally ☐ Credible Witness(es) ☐ Passport ☐ I.D. Card ☐ See Notes	Witness Address	
☐ ID. Issued by ☐ I.D. Number	☐ Expiration Date ☐ Issue Date	Notes	
Signer Signature		Witness Signature	

NOTARY PUBLIC JOURNAL – LARGE ENTRIES | 23

41 | Service: ☐ Acknowledgment ☐ Oath/Affirmation ☐ Jurat ☐ Other/See Notes Fee $_____ Travel_____

Name (print)	Document type /Doc. name	Witness Name (print)	Date and Time Notarized _____ ___ _____ am / pm
Phone # / E-mail	Date of document	Witness Phone # / E-mail	Print of Right Thumb
Address	Satisfactory evidence of ID ☐ Driver's license ☐ Known Personally ☐ Credible Witness(es) ☐ Passport ☐ I.D. Card ☐ See Notes	Witness Address	
☐ ID. Issued by ☐ I.D. Number	☐ Expiration Date ☐ Issue Date	Notes	
Signer Signature		Witness Signature	

42 | Service: ☐ Acknowledgment ☐ Oath/Affirmation ☐ Jurat ☐ Other/See Notes Fee $_____ Travel_____

Name (print)	Document type /Doc. name	Witness Name (print)	Date and Time Notarized _____ ___ _____ am / pm
Phone # / E-mail	Date of document	Witness Phone # / E-mail	Print of Right Thumb
Address	Satisfactory evidence of ID ☐ Driver's license ☐ Known Personally ☐ Credible Witness(es) ☐ Passport ☐ I.D. Card ☐ See Notes	Witness Address	
☐ ID. Issued by ☐ I.D. Number	☐ Expiration Date ☐ Issue Date	Notes	
Signer Signature		Witness Signature	

NOTARY PUBLIC JOURNAL – LARGE ENTRIES

43
Service: ☐ Acknowledgment ☐ Oath/Affirmation ☐ Jurat ☐ Other/See Notes Fee $_____ Travel_____

Name (print)	Document type /Doc. name	Witness Name (print)	Date and Time Notarized _____ ___ _____ am / pm
Phone # / E-mail	Date of document	Witness Phone # / E-mail	Print of Right Thumb
Address	Satisfactory evidence of ID ☐ Driver's license ☐ Known Personally ☐ Credible Witness(es) ☐ Passport ☐ I.D. Card ☐ See Notes	Witness Address	
☐ ID. Issued by ☐ I.D. Number	☐ Expiration Date ☐ Issue Date	Notes	
Signer Signature		Witness Signature	

44
Service: ☐ Acknowledgment ☐ Oath/Affirmation ☐ Jurat ☐ Other/See Notes Fee $_____ Travel_____

Name (print)	Document type /Doc. name	Witness Name (print)	Date and Time Notarized _____ ___ _____ am / pm
Phone # / E-mail	Date of document	Witness Phone # / E-mail	Print of Right Thumb
Address	Satisfactory evidence of ID ☐ Driver's license ☐ Known Personally ☐ Credible Witness(es) ☐ Passport ☐ I.D. Card ☐ See Notes	Witness Address	
☐ ID. Issued by ☐ I.D. Number	☐ Expiration Date ☐ Issue Date	Notes	
Signer Signature		Witness Signature	

NOTARY PUBLIC JOURNAL – LARGE ENTRIES | 25

45 Service: ☐ Acknowledgment ☐ Oath/Affirmation ☐ Jurat ☐ Other/See Notes Fee $_____ Travel_____

Name (print)	Document type /Doc. name	Witness Name (print)	Date and Time Notarized _____ ___ _____ am / pm
Phone # / E-mail	Date of document	Witness Phone # / E-mail	Print of Right Thumb
Address	Satisfactory evidence of ID ☐ Driver's license ☐ Known Personally ☐ Credible Witness(es) ☐ Passport ☐ I.D. Card ☐ See Notes	Witness Address	
☐ ID. Issued by	☐ Expiration Date	Notes	
☐ I.D. Number	☐ Issue Date		
Signer Signature		Witness Signature	

46 Service: ☐ Acknowledgment ☐ Oath/Affirmation ☐ Jurat ☐ Other/See Notes Fee $_____ Travel_____

Name (print)	Document type /Doc. name	Witness Name (print)	Date and Time Notarized _____ ___ _____ am / pm
Phone # / E-mail	Date of document	Witness Phone # / E-mail	Print of Right Thumb
Address	Satisfactory evidence of ID ☐ Driver's license ☐ Known Personally ☐ Credible Witness(es) ☐ Passport ☐ I.D. Card ☐ See Notes	Witness Address	
☐ ID. Issued by	☐ Expiration Date	Notes	
☐ I.D. Number	☐ Issue Date		
Signer Signature		Witness Signature	

26 | NOTARY PUBLIC JOURNAL – LARGE ENTRIES

47
Service: ☐ Acknowledgment ☐ Oath/Affirmation ☐ Jurat ☐ Other/See Notes   Fee $_____   Travel_____

Name (print)	Document type /Doc. name	Witness Name (print)	Date and Time Notarized _____ ___ _____ am / pm
Phone # / E-mail	Date of document	Witness Phone # / E-mail	Print of Right Thumb
Address	Satisfactory evidence of ID ☐ Driver's license ☐ Known Personally ☐ Credible Witness(es) ☐ Passport ☐ I.D. Card ☐ See Notes	Witness Address	
☐ ID. Issued by ☐ I.D. Number	☐ Expiration Date ☐ Issue Date	Notes	
Signer Signature		Witness Signature	

48
Service: ☐ Acknowledgment ☐ Oath/Affirmation ☐ Jurat ☐ Other/See Notes   Fee $_____   Travel_____

Name (print)	Document type /Doc. name	Witness Name (print)	Date and Time Notarized _____ ___ _____ am / pm
Phone # / E-mail	Date of document	Witness Phone # / E-mail	Print of Right Thumb
Address	Satisfactory evidence of ID ☐ Driver's license ☐ Known Personally ☐ Credible Witness(es) ☐ Passport ☐ I.D. Card ☐ See Notes	Witness Address	
☐ ID. Issued by ☐ I.D. Number	☐ Expiration Date ☐ Issue Date	Notes	
Signer Signature		Witness Signature	

NOTARY PUBLIC JOURNAL – LARGE ENTRIES | 27

49 | Service: ☐ Acknowledgment ☐ Oath/Affirmation ☐ Jurat ☐ Other/See Notes Fee $_____ Travel_____

Name (print)	Document type /Doc. name	Witness Name (print)	Date and Time Notarized _____ ___ _____ am / pm
Phone # / E-mail	Date of document	Witness Phone # / E-mail	Print of Right Thumb
Address	Satisfactory evidence of ID ☐ Driver's license ☐ Known Personally ☐ Credible Witness(es) ☐ Passport ☐ I.D. Card ☐ See Notes	Witness Address	
☐ ID. Issued by ☐ I.D. Number	☐ Expiration Date ☐ Issue Date	Notes	
Signer Signature		Witness Signature	

50 | Service: ☐ Acknowledgment ☐ Oath/Affirmation ☐ Jurat ☐ Other/See Notes Fee $_____ Travel_____

Name (print)	Document type /Doc. name	Witness Name (print)	Date and Time Notarized _____ ___ _____ am / pm
Phone # / E-mail	Date of document	Witness Phone # / E-mail	Print of Right Thumb
Address	Satisfactory evidence of ID ☐ Driver's license ☐ Known Personally ☐ Credible Witness(es) ☐ Passport ☐ I.D. Card ☐ See Notes	Witness Address	
☐ ID. Issued by ☐ I.D. Number	☐ Expiration Date ☐ Issue Date	Notes	
Signer Signature		Witness Signature	

NOTARY PUBLIC JOURNAL – LARGE ENTRIES

51
Service: ☐ Acknowledgment ☐ Oath/Affirmation ☐ Jurat ☐ Other/See Notes   Fee $_____ Travel_____

Name (print)	Document type /Doc. name	Witness Name (print)	Date and Time Notarized _____ ___ ___ am / pm
Phone # / E-mail	Date of document	Witness Phone # / E-mail	Print of Right Thumb
Address	Satisfactory evidence of ID ☐ Driver's license ☐ Known Personally ☐ Credible Witness(es) ☐ Passport ☐ I.D. Card ☐ See Notes	Witness Address	
☐ ID. Issued by ☐ I.D. Number	☐ Expiration Date ☐ Issue Date	Notes	
Signer Signature		Witness Signature	

52
Service: ☐ Acknowledgment ☐ Oath/Affirmation ☐ Jurat ☐ Other/See Notes   Fee $_____ Travel_____

Name (print)	Document type /Doc. name	Witness Name (print)	Date and Time Notarized _____ ___ ___ am / pm
Phone # / E-mail	Date of document	Witness Phone # / E-mail	Print of Right Thumb
Address	Satisfactory evidence of ID ☐ Driver's license ☐ Known Personally ☐ Credible Witness(es) ☐ Passport ☐ I.D. Card ☐ See Notes	Witness Address	
☐ ID. Issued by ☐ I.D. Number	☐ Expiration Date ☐ Issue Date	Notes	
Signer Signature		Witness Signature	

53

Service: ☐ Acknowledgment ☐ Oath/Affirmation ☐ Jurat ☐ Other/See Notes   Fee $_____   Travel_____

Name (print)	Document type /Doc. name	Witness Name (print)	Date and Time Notarized _____ ___ _____ am / pm
Phone # / E-mail	Date of document	Witness Phone # / E-mail	Print of Right Thumb
Address	Satisfactory evidence of ID ☐ Driver's license ☐ Known Personally ☐ Credible Witness(es) ☐ Passport ☐ I.D. Card ☐ See Notes	Witness Address	
☐ ID. Issued by ☐ I.D. Number	☐ Expiration Date ☐ Issue Date	Notes	
Signer Signature		Witness Signature	

54

Service: ☐ Acknowledgment ☐ Oath/Affirmation ☐ Jurat ☐ Other/See Notes   Fee $_____   Travel_____

Name (print)	Document type /Doc. name	Witness Name (print)	Date and Time Notarized _____ ___ _____ am / pm
Phone # / E-mail	Date of document	Witness Phone # / E-mail	Print of Right Thumb
Address	Satisfactory evidence of ID ☐ Driver's license ☐ Known Personally ☐ Credible Witness(es) ☐ Passport ☐ I.D. Card ☐ See Notes	Witness Address	
☐ ID. Issued by ☐ I.D. Number	☐ Expiration Date ☐ Issue Date	Notes	
Signer Signature		Witness Signature	

NOTARY PUBLIC JOURNAL – LARGE ENTRIES

55

Service: ☐ Acknowledgment ☐ Oath/Affirmation ☐ Jurat ☐ Other/See Notes Fee $_____ Travel_____

Name (print)	Document type /Doc. name	Witness Name (print)	Date and Time Notarized _____ ____ ____ am / pm
Phone # / E-mail	Date of document	Witness Phone # / E-mail	Print of Right Thumb
Address	Satisfactory evidence of ID ☐ Driver's license ☐ Known Personally ☐ Credible Witness(es) ☐ Passport ☐ I.D. Card ☐ See Notes	Witness Address	
☐ ID. Issued by ☐ I.D. Number	☐ Expiration Date ☐ Issue Date	Notes	
Signer Signature		Witness Signature	

56

Service: ☐ Acknowledgment ☐ Oath/Affirmation ☐ Jurat ☐ Other/See Notes Fee $_____ Travel_____

Name (print)	Document type /Doc. name	Witness Name (print)	Date and Time Notarized _____ ____ ____ am / pm
Phone # / E-mail	Date of document	Witness Phone # / E-mail	Print of Right Thumb
Address	Satisfactory evidence of ID ☐ Driver's license ☐ Known Personally ☐ Credible Witness(es) ☐ Passport ☐ I.D. Card ☐ See Notes	Witness Address	
☐ ID. Issued by ☐ I.D. Number	☐ Expiration Date ☐ Issue Date	Notes	
Signer Signature		Witness Signature	

NOTARY PUBLIC JOURNAL – LARGE ENTRIES | 31

57
Service: ☐ Acknowledgment ☐ Oath/Affirmation ☐ Jurat ☐ Other/See Notes Fee $_____ Travel_____

Name (print)	Document type /Doc. name	Witness Name (print)	Date and Time Notarized _____ ___ _____ am / pm
Phone # / E-mail	Date of document	Witness Phone # / E-mail	Print of Right Thumb
Address	Satisfactory evidence of ID ☐ Driver's license ☐ Known Personally ☐ Credible Witness(es) ☐ Passport ☐ I.D. Card ☐ See Notes	Witness Address	
☐ ID. Issued by ☐ I.D. Number	☐ Expiration Date ☐ Issue Date	Notes	
Signer Signature		Witness Signature	

58
Service: ☐ Acknowledgment ☐ Oath/Affirmation ☐ Jurat ☐ Other/See Notes Fee $_____ Travel_____

Name (print)	Document type /Doc. name	Witness Name (print)	Date and Time Notarized _____ ___ _____ am / pm
Phone # / E-mail	Date of document	Witness Phone # / E-mail	Print of Right Thumb
Address	Satisfactory evidence of ID ☐ Driver's license ☐ Known Personally ☐ Credible Witness(es) ☐ Passport ☐ I.D. Card ☐ See Notes	Witness Address	
☐ ID. Issued by ☐ I.D. Number	☐ Expiration Date ☐ Issue Date	Notes	
Signer Signature		Witness Signature	

59

Service: ☐ Acknowledgment ☐ Oath/Affirmation ☐ Jurat ☐ Other/See Notes   Fee $_____   Travel_____

Name (print)	Document type /Doc. name	Witness Name (print)	Date and Time Notarized
			_____ ___ _____ am / pm
Phone # / E-mail	Date of document	Witness Phone # / E-mail	Print of Right Thumb
Address	Satisfactory evidence of ID ☐ Driver's license ☐ Known Personally ☐ Credible Witness(es) ☐ Passport ☐ I.D. Card ☐ See Notes	Witness Address	
☐ ID. Issued by ☐ I.D. Number	☐ Expiration Date ☐ Issue Date	Notes	
Signer Signature		Witness Signature	

60

Service: ☐ Acknowledgment ☐ Oath/Affirmation ☐ Jurat ☐ Other/See Notes   Fee $_____   Travel_____

Name (print)	Document type /Doc. name	Witness Name (print)	Date and Time Notarized
			_____ ___ _____ am / pm
Phone # / E-mail	Date of document	Witness Phone # / E-mail	Print of Right Thumb
Address	Satisfactory evidence of ID ☐ Driver's license ☐ Known Personally ☐ Credible Witness(es) ☐ Passport ☐ I.D. Card ☐ See Notes	Witness Address	
☐ ID. Issued by ☐ I.D. Number	☐ Expiration Date ☐ Issue Date	Notes	
Signer Signature		Witness Signature	

61

Service: ☐ Acknowledgment ☐ Oath/Affirmation ☐ Jurat ☐ Other/See Notes Fee $_____ Travel_____			
Name (print)	Document type /Doc. name	Witness Name (print)	Date and Time Notarized _____ ___ ___ am / pm
Phone # / E-mail	Date of document	Witness Phone # / E-mail	Print of Right Thumb
Address	Satisfactory evidence of ID ☐ Driver's license ☐ Known Personally ☐ Credible Witness(es) ☐ Passport ☐ I.D. Card ☐ See Notes	Witness Address	
☐ ID. Issued by ☐ I.D. Number	☐ Expiration Date ☐ Issue Date	Notes	
Signer Signature		Witness Signature	

62

Service: ☐ Acknowledgment ☐ Oath/Affirmation ☐ Jurat ☐ Other/See Notes Fee $_____ Travel_____			
Name (print)	Document type /Doc. name	Witness Name (print)	Date and Time Notarized _____ ___ ___ am / pm
Phone # / E-mail	Date of document	Witness Phone # / E-mail	Print of Right Thumb
Address	Satisfactory evidence of ID ☐ Driver's license ☐ Known Personally ☐ Credible Witness(es) ☐ Passport ☐ I.D. Card ☐ See Notes	Witness Address	
☐ ID. Issued by ☐ I.D. Number	☐ Expiration Date ☐ Issue Date	Notes	
Signer Signature		Witness Signature	

34 NOTARY PUBLIC JOURNAL – LARGE ENTRIES

63

Service: ☐ Acknowledgment ☐ Oath/Affirmation ☐ Jurat ☐ Other/See Notes Fee $_____ Travel_____

Name (print)	Document type /Doc. name	Witness Name (print)	Date and Time Notarized _____ ___ _____ am / pm
Phone # / E-mail	Date of document	Witness Phone # / E-mail	Print of Right Thumb
Address	Satisfactory evidence of ID ☐ Driver's license ☐ Known Personally ☐ Credible Witness(es) ☐ Passport ☐ I.D. Card ☐ See Notes	Witness Address	
☐ ID. Issued by ☐ I.D. Number	☐ Expiration Date ☐ Issue Date	Notes	
Signer Signature		Witness Signature	

64

Service: ☐ Acknowledgment ☐ Oath/Affirmation ☐ Jurat ☐ Other/See Notes Fee $_____ Travel_____

Name (print)	Document type /Doc. name	Witness Name (print)	Date and Time Notarized _____ ___ _____ am / pm
Phone # / E-mail	Date of document	Witness Phone # / E-mail	Print of Right Thumb
Address	Satisfactory evidence of ID ☐ Driver's license ☐ Known Personally ☐ Credible Witness(es) ☐ Passport ☐ I.D. Card ☐ See Notes	Witness Address	
☐ ID. Issued by ☐ I.D. Number	☐ Expiration Date ☐ Issue Date	Notes	
Signer Signature		Witness Signature	

65

Service: ☐ Acknowledgment ☐ Oath/Affirmation ☐ Jurat ☐ Other/See Notes   Fee $_____   Travel_____

Name (print)	Document type /Doc. name	Witness Name (print)	Date and Time Notarized _____ ___ _____ am / pm
Phone # / E-mail	Date of document	Witness Phone # / E-mail	Print of Right Thumb
Address	Satisfactory evidence of ID ☐ Driver's license ☐ Known Personally ☐ Credible Witness(es) ☐ Passport ☐ I.D. Card ☐ See Notes	Witness Address	
☐ ID. Issued by ☐ I.D. Number	☐ Expiration Date ☐ Issue Date	Notes	
Signer Signature		Witness Signature	

66

Service: ☐ Acknowledgment ☐ Oath/Affirmation ☐ Jurat ☐ Other/See Notes   Fee $_____   Travel_____

Name (print)	Document type /Doc. name	Witness Name (print)	Date and Time Notarized _____ ___ _____ am / pm
Phone # / E-mail	Date of document	Witness Phone # / E-mail	Print of Right Thumb
Address	Satisfactory evidence of ID ☐ Driver's license ☐ Known Personally ☐ Credible Witness(es) ☐ Passport ☐ I.D. Card ☐ See Notes	Witness Address	
☐ ID. Issued by ☐ I.D. Number	☐ Expiration Date ☐ Issue Date	Notes	
Signer Signature		Witness Signature	

67

Service: ☐ Acknowledgment ☐ Oath/Affirmation ☐ Jurat ☐ Other/See Notes Fee $_____ Travel_____

Name (print)	Document type /Doc. name	Witness Name (print)	Date and Time Notarized _____ ___ ___ am / pm
Phone # / E-mail	Date of document	Witness Phone # / E-mail	Print of Right Thumb
Address	Satisfactory evidence of ID ☐ Driver's license ☐ Known Personally ☐ Credible Witness(es) ☐ Passport ☐ I.D. Card ☐ See Notes	Witness Address	
☐ ID. Issued by ☐ I.D. Number	☐ Expiration Date ☐ Issue Date	Notes	
Signer Signature		Witness Signature	

68

Service: ☐ Acknowledgment ☐ Oath/Affirmation ☐ Jurat ☐ Other/See Notes Fee $_____ Travel_____

Name (print)	Document type /Doc. name	Witness Name (print)	Date and Time Notarized _____ ___ ___ am / pm
Phone # / E-mail	Date of document	Witness Phone # / E-mail	Print of Right Thumb
Address	Satisfactory evidence of ID ☐ Driver's license ☐ Known Personally ☐ Credible Witness(es) ☐ Passport ☐ I.D. Card ☐ See Notes	Witness Address	
☐ ID. Issued by ☐ I.D. Number	☐ Expiration Date ☐ Issue Date	Notes	
Signer Signature		Witness Signature	

NOTARY PUBLIC JOURNAL – LARGE ENTRIES | 37

69 | Service: ☐ Acknowledgment ☐ Oath/Affirmation ☐ Jurat ☐ Other/See Notes Fee $_____ Travel_____

Name (print)	Document type /Doc. name	Witness Name (print)	Date and Time Notarized _____ ___ _____ am / pm
Phone # / E-mail	Date of document	Witness Phone # / E-mail	Print of Right Thumb
Address	Satisfactory evidence of ID ☐ Driver's license ☐ Known Personally ☐ Credible Witness(es) ☐ Passport ☐ I.D. Card ☐ See Notes	Witness Address	
☐ ID. Issued by ☐ I.D. Number	☐ Expiration Date ☐ Issue Date	Notes	
Signer Signature		Witness Signature	

70 | Service: ☐ Acknowledgment ☐ Oath/Affirmation ☐ Jurat ☐ Other/See Notes Fee $_____ Travel_____

Name (print)	Document type /Doc. name	Witness Name (print)	Date and Time Notarized _____ ___ _____ am / pm
Phone # / E-mail	Date of document	Witness Phone # / E-mail	Print of Right Thumb
Address	Satisfactory evidence of ID ☐ Driver's license ☐ Known Personally ☐ Credible Witness(es) ☐ Passport ☐ I.D. Card ☐ See Notes	Witness Address	
☐ ID. Issued by ☐ I.D. Number	☐ Expiration Date ☐ Issue Date	Notes	
Signer Signature		Witness Signature	

38 | NOTARY PUBLIC JOURNAL – LARGE ENTRIES

71 — Service: ☐ Acknowledgment ☐ Oath/Affirmation ☐ Jurat ☐ Other/See Notes   Fee $_____   Travel_____

Name (print)	Document type /Doc. name	Witness Name (print)	Date and Time Notarized _____ ___ ___ am / pm
Phone # / E-mail	Date of document	Witness Phone # / E-mail	Print of Right Thumb
Address	Satisfactory evidence of ID ☐ Driver's license ☐ Known Personally ☐ Credible Witness(es) ☐ Passport ☐ I.D. Card ☐ See Notes	Witness Address	
☐ ID. Issued by ☐ I.D. Number	☐ Expiration Date ☐ Issue Date	Notes	
Signer Signature		Witness Signature	

72 — Service: ☐ Acknowledgment ☐ Oath/Affirmation ☐ Jurat ☐ Other/See Notes   Fee $_____   Travel_____

Name (print)	Document type /Doc. name	Witness Name (print)	Date and Time Notarized _____ ___ ___ am / pm
Phone # / E-mail	Date of document	Witness Phone # / E-mail	Print of Right Thumb
Address	Satisfactory evidence of ID ☐ Driver's license ☐ Known Personally ☐ Credible Witness(es) ☐ Passport ☐ I.D. Card ☐ See Notes	Witness Address	
☐ ID. Issued by ☐ I.D. Number	☐ Expiration Date ☐ Issue Date	Notes	
Signer Signature		Witness Signature	

NOTARY PUBLIC JOURNAL – LARGE ENTRIES | 39

73 — Service: ☐ Acknowledgment ☐ Oath/Affirmation ☐ Jurat ☐ Other/See Notes   Fee $_____   Travel_____

Name (print)	Document type /Doc. name	Witness Name (print)	Date and Time Notarized _____ ___ _____ am / pm
Phone # / E-mail	Date of document	Witness Phone # / E-mail	Print of Right Thumb
Address	Satisfactory evidence of ID ☐ Driver's license ☐ Known Personally ☐ Credible Witness(es) ☐ Passport ☐ I.D. Card ☐ See Notes	Witness Address	
☐ ID. Issued by ☐ I.D. Number	☐ Expiration Date ☐ Issue Date	Notes	
Signer Signature		Witness Signature	

74 — Service: ☐ Acknowledgment ☐ Oath/Affirmation ☐ Jurat ☐ Other/See Notes   Fee $_____   Travel_____

Name (print)	Document type /Doc. name	Witness Name (print)	Date and Time Notarized _____ ___ _____ am / pm
Phone # / E-mail	Date of document	Witness Phone # / E-mail	Print of Right Thumb
Address	Satisfactory evidence of ID ☐ Driver's license ☐ Known Personally ☐ Credible Witness(es) ☐ Passport ☐ I.D. Card ☐ See Notes	Witness Address	
☐ ID. Issued by ☐ I.D. Number	☐ Expiration Date ☐ Issue Date	Notes	
Signer Signature		Witness Signature	

40 | NOTARY PUBLIC JOURNAL – LARGE ENTRIES

75 — Service: ☐ Acknowledgment ☐ Oath/Affirmation ☐ Jurat ☐ Other/See Notes   Fee $_____   Travel_____

Name (print)	Document type /Doc. name	Witness Name (print)	Date and Time Notarized _____ ___ _____ am / pm
Phone # / E-mail	Date of document	Witness Phone # / E-mail	Print of Right Thumb
Address	Satisfactory evidence of ID ☐ Driver's license ☐ Known Personally ☐ Credible Witness(es) ☐ Passport ☐ I.D. Card ☐ See Notes	Witness Address	
☐ ID. Issued by ☐ I.D. Number	☐ Expiration Date ☐ Issue Date	Notes	
Signer Signature		Witness Signature	

76 — Service: ☐ Acknowledgment ☐ Oath/Affirmation ☐ Jurat ☐ Other/See Notes   Fee $_____   Travel_____

Name (print)	Document type /Doc. name	Witness Name (print)	Date and Time Notarized _____ ___ _____ am / pm
Phone # / E-mail	Date of document	Witness Phone # / E-mail	Print of Right Thumb
Address	Satisfactory evidence of ID ☐ Driver's license ☐ Known Personally ☐ Credible Witness(es) ☐ Passport ☐ I.D. Card ☐ See Notes	Witness Address	
☐ ID. Issued by ☐ I.D. Number	☐ Expiration Date ☐ Issue Date	Notes	
Signer Signature		Witness Signature	

77

Service: ☐ Acknowledgment ☐ Oath/Affirmation ☐ Jurat ☐ Other/See Notes   Fee $_____ Travel_____

Name (print)	Document type /Doc. name	Witness Name (print)	Date and Time Notarized _____ __ _____ am / pm
Phone # / E-mail	Date of document	Witness Phone # / E-mail	Print of Right Thumb
Address	Satisfactory evidence of ID ☐ Driver's license ☐ Known Personally ☐ Credible Witness(es) ☐ Passport ☐ I.D. Card ☐ See Notes	Witness Address	
☐ ID. Issued by ☐ I.D. Number	☐ Expiration Date ☐ Issue Date	Notes	
Signer Signature		Witness Signature	

78

Service: ☐ Acknowledgment ☐ Oath/Affirmation ☐ Jurat ☐ Other/See Notes   Fee $_____ Travel_____

Name (print)	Document type /Doc. name	Witness Name (print)	Date and Time Notarized _____ __ _____ am / pm
Phone # / E-mail	Date of document	Witness Phone # / E-mail	Print of Right Thumb
Address	Satisfactory evidence of ID ☐ Driver's license ☐ Known Personally ☐ Credible Witness(es) ☐ Passport ☐ I.D. Card ☐ See Notes	Witness Address	
☐ ID. Issued by ☐ I.D. Number	☐ Expiration Date ☐ Issue Date	Notes	
Signer Signature		Witness Signature	

42 | NOTARY PUBLIC JOURNAL – LARGE ENTRIES

79

Service: ☐ Acknowledgment ☐ Oath/Affirmation ☐ Jurat ☐ Other/See Notes   Fee $_____ Travel_____

Name (print)	Document type /Doc. name	Witness Name (print)	Date and Time Notarized _____ ___ _____ am / pm
Phone # / E-mail	Date of document	Witness Phone # / E-mail	Print of Right Thumb
Address	Satisfactory evidence of ID ☐ Driver's license ☐ Known Personally ☐ Credible Witness(es) ☐ Passport ☐ I.D. Card ☐ See Notes	Witness Address	
☐ ID. Issued by ☐ I.D. Number	☐ Expiration Date ☐ Issue Date	Notes	
Signer Signature		Witness Signature	

80

Service: ☐ Acknowledgment ☐ Oath/Affirmation ☐ Jurat ☐ Other/See Notes   Fee $_____ Travel_____

Name (print)	Document type /Doc. name	Witness Name (print)	Date and Time Notarized _____ ___ _____ am / pm
Phone # / E-mail	Date of document	Witness Phone # / E-mail	Print of Right Thumb
Address	Satisfactory evidence of ID ☐ Driver's license ☐ Known Personally ☐ Credible Witness(es) ☐ Passport ☐ I.D. Card ☐ See Notes	Witness Address	
☐ ID. Issued by ☐ I.D. Number	☐ Expiration Date ☐ Issue Date	Notes	
Signer Signature		Witness Signature	

NOTARY PUBLIC JOURNAL – LARGE ENTRIES | 43

81
Service: ☐ Acknowledgment ☐ Oath/Affirmation ☐ Jurat ☐ Other/See Notes Fee $_____ Travel_____

Name (print)	Document type /Doc. name	Witness Name (print)	Date and Time Notarized _____ ___ _____ am / pm
Phone # / E-mail	Date of document	Witness Phone # / E-mail	Print of Right Thumb
Address	Satisfactory evidence of ID ☐ Driver's license ☐ Known Personally ☐ Credible Witness(es) ☐ Passport ☐ I.D. Card ☐ See Notes	Witness Address	
☐ ID. Issued by ☐ I.D. Number	☐ Expiration Date ☐ Issue Date	Notes	
Signer Signature		Witness Signature	

82
Service: ☐ Acknowledgment ☐ Oath/Affirmation ☐ Jurat ☐ Other/See Notes Fee $_____ Travel_____

Name (print)	Document type /Doc. name	Witness Name (print)	Date and Time Notarized _____ ___ _____ am / pm
Phone # / E-mail	Date of document	Witness Phone # / E-mail	Print of Right Thumb
Address	Satisfactory evidence of ID ☐ Driver's license ☐ Known Personally ☐ Credible Witness(es) ☐ Passport ☐ I.D. Card ☐ See Notes	Witness Address	
☐ ID. Issued by ☐ I.D. Number	☐ Expiration Date ☐ Issue Date	Notes	
Signer Signature		Witness Signature	

83

Service: ☐ Acknowledgment ☐ Oath/Affirmation ☐ Jurat ☐ Other/See Notes Fee $_____ Travel_____

Name (print)	Document type /Doc. name	Witness Name (print)	Date and Time Notarized _____ ___ _____ am / pm
Phone # / E-mail	Date of document	Witness Phone # / E-mail	Print of Right Thumb
Address	Satisfactory evidence of ID ☐ Driver's license ☐ Known Personally ☐ Credible Witness(es) ☐ Passport ☐ I.D. Card ☐ See Notes	Witness Address	
☐ ID. Issued by ☐ I.D. Number	☐ Expiration Date ☐ Issue Date	Notes	
Signer Signature		Witness Signature	

84

Service: ☐ Acknowledgment ☐ Oath/Affirmation ☐ Jurat ☐ Other/See Notes Fee $_____ Travel_____

Name (print)	Document type /Doc. name	Witness Name (print)	Date and Time Notarized _____ ___ _____ am / pm
Phone # / E-mail	Date of document	Witness Phone # / E-mail	Print of Right Thumb
Address	Satisfactory evidence of ID ☐ Driver's license ☐ Known Personally ☐ Credible Witness(es) ☐ Passport ☐ I.D. Card ☐ See Notes	Witness Address	
☐ ID. Issued by ☐ I.D. Number	☐ Expiration Date ☐ Issue Date	Notes	
Signer Signature		Witness Signature	

85

Service: ☐ Acknowledgment ☐ Oath/Affirmation ☐ Jurat ☐ Other/See Notes   Fee $_____   Travel_____

Name (print)	Document type /Doc. name	Witness Name (print)	Date and Time Notarized _____ ___ ___ am / pm
Phone # / E-mail	Date of document	Witness Phone # / E-mail	Print of Right Thumb
Address	Satisfactory evidence of ID ☐ Driver's license ☐ Known Personally ☐ Credible Witness(es) ☐ Passport ☐ I.D. Card ☐ See Notes	Witness Address	
☐ ID. Issued by ☐ I.D. Number	☐ Expiration Date ☐ Issue Date	Notes	
Signer Signature		Witness Signature	

86

Service: ☐ Acknowledgment ☐ Oath/Affirmation ☐ Jurat ☐ Other/See Notes   Fee $_____   Travel_____

Name (print)	Document type /Doc. name	Witness Name (print)	Date and Time Notarized _____ ___ ___ am / pm
Phone # / E-mail	Date of document	Witness Phone # / E-mail	Print of Right Thumb
Address	Satisfactory evidence of ID ☐ Driver's license ☐ Known Personally ☐ Credible Witness(es) ☐ Passport ☐ I.D. Card ☐ See Notes	Witness Address	
☐ ID. Issued by ☐ I.D. Number	☐ Expiration Date ☐ Issue Date	Notes	
Signer Signature		Witness Signature	

NOTARY PUBLIC JOURNAL – LARGE ENTRIES

87
Service: ☐ Acknowledgment ☐ Oath/Affirmation ☐ Jurat ☐ Other/See Notes   Fee $_____ Travel_____

Name (print)	Document type /Doc. name	Witness Name (print)	Date and Time Notarized _____ ___ ___ am / pm
Phone # / E-mail	Date of document	Witness Phone # / E-mail	Print of Right Thumb
Address	Satisfactory evidence of ID ☐ Driver's license ☐ Known Personally ☐ Credible Witness(es) ☐ Passport ☐ I.D. Card ☐ See Notes	Witness Address	
☐ ID. Issued by	☐ Expiration Date	Notes	
☐ I.D. Number	☐ Issue Date		
Signer Signature		Witness Signature	

88
Service: ☐ Acknowledgment ☐ Oath/Affirmation ☐ Jurat ☐ Other/See Notes   Fee $_____ Travel_____

Name (print)	Document type /Doc. name	Witness Name (print)	Date and Time Notarized _____ ___ ___ am / pm
Phone # / E-mail	Date of document	Witness Phone # / E-mail	Print of Right Thumb
Address	Satisfactory evidence of ID ☐ Driver's license ☐ Known Personally ☐ Credible Witness(es) ☐ Passport ☐ I.D. Card ☐ See Notes	Witness Address	
☐ ID. Issued by	☐ Expiration Date	Notes	
☐ I.D. Number	☐ Issue Date		
Signer Signature		Witness Signature	

89

Service: ☐ Acknowledgment ☐ Oath/Affirmation ☐ Jurat ☐ Other/See Notes   Fee $_____   Travel_____

Name (print)	Document type /Doc. name	Witness Name (print)	Date and Time Notarized _____ ___ _____ am / pm
Phone # / E-mail	Date of document	Witness Phone # / E-mail	Print of Right Thumb
Address	Satisfactory evidence of ID ☐ Driver's license ☐ Known Personally ☐ Credible Witness(es) ☐ Passport ☐ I.D. Card ☐ See Notes	Witness Address	
☐ ID. Issued by ☐ I.D. Number	☐ Expiration Date ☐ Issue Date	Notes	
Signer Signature		Witness Signature	

90

Service: ☐ Acknowledgment ☐ Oath/Affirmation ☐ Jurat ☐ Other/See Notes   Fee $_____   Travel_____

Name (print)	Document type /Doc. name	Witness Name (print)	Date and Time Notarized _____ ___ _____ am / pm
Phone # / E-mail	Date of document	Witness Phone # / E-mail	Print of Right Thumb
Address	Satisfactory evidence of ID ☐ Driver's license ☐ Known Personally ☐ Credible Witness(es) ☐ Passport ☐ I.D. Card ☐ See Notes	Witness Address	
☐ ID. Issued by ☐ I.D. Number	☐ Expiration Date ☐ Issue Date	Notes	
Signer Signature		Witness Signature	

48 NOTARY PUBLIC JOURNAL – LARGE ENTRIES

91 Service: ☐ Acknowledgment ☐ Oath/Affirmation ☐ Jurat ☐ Other/See Notes Fee $_____ Travel_____

Name (print)	Document type /Doc. name	Witness Name (print)	Date and Time Notarized ____ ___ ___ am / pm
Phone # / E-mail	Date of document	Witness Phone # / E-mail	Print of Right Thumb
Address	Satisfactory evidence of ID ☐ Driver's license ☐ Known Personally ☐ Credible Witness(es) ☐ Passport ☐ I.D. Card ☐ See Notes	Witness Address	
☐ ID. Issued by ☐ I.D. Number	☐ Expiration Date ☐ Issue Date	Notes	
Signer Signature		Witness Signature	

92 Service: ☐ Acknowledgment ☐ Oath/Affirmation ☐ Jurat ☐ Other/See Notes Fee $_____ Travel_____

Name (print)	Document type /Doc. name	Witness Name (print)	Date and Time Notarized ____ ___ ___ am / pm
Phone # / E-mail	Date of document	Witness Phone # / E-mail	Print of Right Thumb
Address	Satisfactory evidence of ID ☐ Driver's license ☐ Known Personally ☐ Credible Witness(es) ☐ Passport ☐ I.D. Card ☐ See Notes	Witness Address	
☐ ID. Issued by ☐ I.D. Number	☐ Expiration Date ☐ Issue Date	Notes	
Signer Signature		Witness Signature	

NOTARY PUBLIC JOURNAL – LARGE ENTRIES | 49

93

Service: ☐ Acknowledgment ☐ Oath/Affirmation ☐ Jurat ☐ Other/See Notes Fee $_____ Travel_____

Name (print)	Document type /Doc. name	Witness Name (print)	Date and Time Notarized _____ ___ _____ am / pm
Phone # / E-mail	Date of document	Witness Phone # / E-mail	Print of Right Thumb
Address	Satisfactory evidence of ID ☐ Driver's license ☐ Known Personally ☐ Credible Witness(es) ☐ Passport ☐ I.D. Card ☐ See Notes	Witness Address	
☐ ID. Issued by ☐ I.D. Number	☐ Expiration Date ☐ Issue Date	Notes	
Signer Signature		Witness Signature	

94

Service: ☐ Acknowledgment ☐ Oath/Affirmation ☐ Jurat ☐ Other/See Notes Fee $_____ Travel_____

Name (print)	Document type /Doc. name	Witness Name (print)	Date and Time Notarized _____ ___ _____ am / pm
Phone # / E-mail	Date of document	Witness Phone # / E-mail	Print of Right Thumb
Address	Satisfactory evidence of ID ☐ Driver's license ☐ Known Personally ☐ Credible Witness(es) ☐ Passport ☐ I.D. Card ☐ See Notes	Witness Address	
☐ ID. Issued by ☐ I.D. Number	☐ Expiration Date ☐ Issue Date	Notes	
Signer Signature		Witness Signature	

50 | NOTARY PUBLIC JOURNAL – LARGE ENTRIES

95 Service: ☐ Acknowledgment ☐ Oath/Affirmation ☐ Jurat ☐ Other/See Notes   Fee $_____   Travel_____

Name (print)	Document type /Doc. name	Witness Name (print)	Date and Time Notarized _____ ___ _____ am / pm
Phone # / E-mail	Date of document	Witness Phone # / E-mail	Print of Right Thumb
Address	Satisfactory evidence of ID ☐ Driver's license ☐ Known Personally ☐ Credible Witness(es) ☐ Passport ☐ I.D. Card ☐ See Notes	Witness Address	
☐ ID. Issued by ☐ I.D. Number	☐ Expiration Date ☐ Issue Date	Notes	
Signer Signature		Witness Signature	

96 Service: ☐ Acknowledgment ☐ Oath/Affirmation ☐ Jurat ☐ Other/See Notes   Fee $_____   Travel_____

Name (print)	Document type /Doc. name	Witness Name (print)	Date and Time Notarized _____ ___ _____ am / pm
Phone # / E-mail	Date of document	Witness Phone # / E-mail	Print of Right Thumb
Address	Satisfactory evidence of ID ☐ Driver's license ☐ Known Personally ☐ Credible Witness(es) ☐ Passport ☐ I.D. Card ☐ See Notes	Witness Address	
☐ ID. Issued by ☐ I.D. Number	☐ Expiration Date ☐ Issue Date	Notes	
Signer Signature		Witness Signature	

NOTARY PUBLIC JOURNAL – LARGE ENTRIES | 51

97
Service: ☐ Acknowledgment ☐ Oath/Affirmation ☐ Jurat ☐ Other/See Notes   Fee $_____   Travel_____

Name (print)	Document type /Doc. name	Witness Name (print)	Date and Time Notarized _____ ___ _____ am / pm
Phone # / E-mail	Date of document	Witness Phone # / E-mail	Print of Right Thumb
Address	Satisfactory evidence of ID ☐ Driver's license ☐ Known Personally ☐ Credible Witness(es) ☐ Passport ☐ I.D. Card ☐ See Notes	Witness Address	
☐ ID. Issued by ☐ I.D. Number	☐ Expiration Date ☐ Issue Date	Notes	
Signer Signature		Witness Signature	

98
Service: ☐ Acknowledgment ☐ Oath/Affirmation ☐ Jurat ☐ Other/See Notes   Fee $_____   Travel_____

Name (print)	Document type /Doc. name	Witness Name (print)	Date and Time Notarized _____ ___ _____ am / pm
Phone # / E-mail	Date of document	Witness Phone # / E-mail	Print of Right Thumb
Address	Satisfactory evidence of ID ☐ Driver's license ☐ Known Personally ☐ Credible Witness(es) ☐ Passport ☐ I.D. Card ☐ See Notes	Witness Address	
☐ ID. Issued by ☐ I.D. Number	☐ Expiration Date ☐ Issue Date	Notes	
Signer Signature		Witness Signature	

52 | NOTARY PUBLIC JOURNAL – LARGE ENTRIES

99 | Service: ☐ Acknowledgment ☐ Oath/Affirmation ☐ Jurat ☐ Other/See Notes Fee $_____ Travel_____

Name (print)	Document type /Doc. name	Witness Name (print)	Date and Time Notarized _____ ___ _____ am / pm
Phone # / E-mail	Date of document	Witness Phone # / E-mail	Print of Right Thumb
Address	Satisfactory evidence of ID ☐ Driver's license ☐ Known Personally ☐ Credible Witness(es) ☐ Passport ☐ I.D. Card ☐ See Notes	Witness Address	
☐ ID. Issued by ☐ I.D. Number	☐ Expiration Date ☐ Issue Date	Notes	
Signer Signature		Witness Signature	

100 | Service: ☐ Acknowledgment ☐ Oath/Affirmation ☐ Jurat ☐ Other/See Notes Fee $_____ Travel_____

Name (print)	Document type /Doc. name	Witness Name (print)	Date and Time Notarized _____ ___ _____ am / pm
Phone # / E-mail	Date of document	Witness Phone # / E-mail	Print of Right Thumb
Address	Satisfactory evidence of ID ☐ Driver's license ☐ Known Personally ☐ Credible Witness(es) ☐ Passport ☐ I.D. Card ☐ See Notes	Witness Address	
☐ ID. Issued by ☐ I.D. Number	☐ Expiration Date ☐ Issue Date	Notes	
Signer Signature		Witness Signature	

NOTARY PUBLIC JOURNAL – LARGE ENTRIES

101
Service: ☐ Acknowledgment ☐ Oath/Affirmation ☐ Jurat ☐ Other/See Notes   Fee $_____   Travel_____

Name (print)	Document type /Doc. name	Witness Name (print)	Date and Time Notarized _____ ___ _____ am / pm
Phone # / E-mail	Date of document	Witness Phone # / E-mail	Print of Right Thumb
Address	Satisfactory evidence of ID ☐ Driver's license ☐ Known Personally ☐ Credible Witness(es) ☐ Passport ☐ I.D. Card ☐ See Notes	Witness Address	
☐ ID. Issued by ☐ I.D. Number	☐ Expiration Date ☐ Issue Date	Notes	
Signer Signature		Witness Signature	

102
Service: ☐ Acknowledgment ☐ Oath/Affirmation ☐ Jurat ☐ Other/See Notes   Fee $_____   Travel_____

Name (print)	Document type /Doc. name	Witness Name (print)	Date and Time Notarized _____ ___ _____ am / pm
Phone # / E-mail	Date of document	Witness Phone # / E-mail	Print of Right Thumb
Address	Satisfactory evidence of ID ☐ Driver's license ☐ Known Personally ☐ Credible Witness(es) ☐ Passport ☐ I.D. Card ☐ See Notes	Witness Address	
☐ ID. Issued by ☐ I.D. Number	☐ Expiration Date ☐ Issue Date	Notes	
Signer Signature		Witness Signature	

54 NOTARY PUBLIC JOURNAL – LARGE ENTRIES

103 Service: ☐ Acknowledgment ☐ Oath/Affirmation ☐ Jurat ☐ Other/See Notes   Fee $_____ Travel_____

Name (print)	Document type /Doc. name	Witness Name (print)	Date and Time Notarized _____ ____ ____ am / pm
Phone # / E-mail	Date of document	Witness Phone # / E-mail	Print of Right Thumb
Address	Satisfactory evidence of ID ☐ Driver's license ☐ Known Personally ☐ Credible Witness(es) ☐ Passport ☐ I.D. Card ☐ See Notes	Witness Address	
☐ ID. Issued by ☐ I.D. Number	☐ Expiration Date ☐ Issue Date	Notes	
Signer Signature		Witness Signature	

104 Service: ☐ Acknowledgment ☐ Oath/Affirmation ☐ Jurat ☐ Other/See Notes   Fee $_____ Travel_____

Name (print)	Document type /Doc. name	Witness Name (print)	Date and Time Notarized _____ ____ ____ am / pm
Phone # / E-mail	Date of document	Witness Phone # / E-mail	Print of Right Thumb
Address	Satisfactory evidence of ID ☐ Driver's license ☐ Known Personally ☐ Credible Witness(es) ☐ Passport ☐ I.D. Card ☐ See Notes	Witness Address	
☐ ID. Issued by ☐ I.D. Number	☐ Expiration Date ☐ Issue Date	Notes	
Signer Signature		Witness Signature	

NOTARY PUBLIC JOURNAL – LARGE ENTRIES | 55

105
Service: ☐ Acknowledgment ☐ Oath/Affirmation ☐ Jurat ☐ Other/See Notes   Fee $_____   Travel_____

Name (print)	Document type /Doc. name	Witness Name (print)	Date and Time Notarized _____ ___ _____ am / pm
Phone # / E-mail	Date of document	Witness Phone # / E-mail	Print of Right Thumb
Address	Satisfactory evidence of ID ☐ Driver's license ☐ Known Personally ☐ Credible Witness(es) ☐ Passport ☐ I.D. Card ☐ See Notes	Witness Address	
☐ ID. Issued by ☐ I.D. Number	☐ Expiration Date ☐ Issue Date	Notes	
Signer Signature		Witness Signature	

106
Service: ☐ Acknowledgment ☐ Oath/Affirmation ☐ Jurat ☐ Other/See Notes   Fee $_____   Travel_____

Name (print)	Document type /Doc. name	Witness Name (print)	Date and Time Notarized _____ ___ _____ am / pm
Phone # / E-mail	Date of document	Witness Phone # / E-mail	Print of Right Thumb
Address	Satisfactory evidence of ID ☐ Driver's license ☐ Known Personally ☐ Credible Witness(es) ☐ Passport ☐ I.D. Card ☐ See Notes	Witness Address	
☐ ID. Issued by ☐ I.D. Number	☐ Expiration Date ☐ Issue Date	Notes	
Signer Signature		Witness Signature	

107

Service: ☐ Acknowledgment ☐ Oath/Affirmation ☐ Jurat ☐ Other/See Notes   Fee $_____ Travel_____

Name (print)	Document type /Doc. name	Witness Name (print)	Date and Time Notarized _____ ____ _____ am / pm
Phone # / E-mail	Date of document	Witness Phone # / E-mail	Print of Right Thumb
Address	Satisfactory evidence of ID ☐ Driver's license ☐ Known Personally ☐ Credible Witness(es) ☐ Passport ☐ I.D. Card ☐ See Notes	Witness Address	
☐ ID. Issued by ☐ I.D. Number	☐ Expiration Date ☐ Issue Date	Notes	
Signer Signature		Witness Signature	

108

Service: ☐ Acknowledgment ☐ Oath/Affirmation ☐ Jurat ☐ Other/See Notes   Fee $_____ Travel_____

Name (print)	Document type /Doc. name	Witness Name (print)	Date and Time Notarized _____ ____ _____ am / pm
Phone # / E-mail	Date of document	Witness Phone # / E-mail	Print of Right Thumb
Address	Satisfactory evidence of ID ☐ Driver's license ☐ Known Personally ☐ Credible Witness(es) ☐ Passport ☐ I.D. Card ☐ See Notes	Witness Address	
☐ ID. Issued by ☐ I.D. Number	☐ Expiration Date ☐ Issue Date	Notes	
Signer Signature		Witness Signature	

NOTARY PUBLIC JOURNAL – LARGE ENTRIES

109

Service: ☐ Acknowledgment ☐ Oath/Affirmation ☐ Jurat ☐ Other/See Notes Fee $_____ Travel_____

Name (print)	Document type /Doc. name	Witness Name (print)	Date and Time Notarized _____ ___ _____ am / pm
Phone # / E-mail	Date of document	Witness Phone # / E-mail	Print of Right Thumb
Address	Satisfactory evidence of ID ☐ Driver's license ☐ Known Personally ☐ Credible Witness(es) ☐ Passport ☐ I.D. Card ☐ See Notes	Witness Address	
☐ ID. Issued by ☐ I.D. Number	☐ Expiration Date ☐ Issue Date	Notes	
Signer Signature		Witness Signature	

110

Service: ☐ Acknowledgment ☐ Oath/Affirmation ☐ Jurat ☐ Other/See Notes Fee $_____ Travel_____

Name (print)	Document type /Doc. name	Witness Name (print)	Date and Time Notarized _____ ___ _____ am / pm
Phone # / E-mail	Date of document	Witness Phone # / E-mail	Print of Right Thumb
Address	Satisfactory evidence of ID ☐ Driver's license ☐ Known Personally ☐ Credible Witness(es) ☐ Passport ☐ I.D. Card ☐ See Notes	Witness Address	
☐ ID. Issued by ☐ I.D. Number	☐ Expiration Date ☐ Issue Date	Notes	
Signer Signature		Witness Signature	

58 | NOTARY PUBLIC JOURNAL – LARGE ENTRIES

111 Service: ☐ Acknowledgment ☐ Oath/Affirmation ☐ Jurat ☐ Other/See Notes Fee $_____ Travel_____

Name (print)	Document type /Doc. name	Witness Name (print)	Date and Time Notarized _____ ___ ___ am / pm
Phone # / E-mail	Date of document	Witness Phone # / E-mail	Print of Right Thumb
Address	Satisfactory evidence of ID ☐ Driver's license ☐ Known Personally ☐ Credible Witness(es) ☐ Passport ☐ I.D. Card ☐ See Notes	Witness Address	
☐ ID. Issued by ☐ I.D. Number	☐ Expiration Date ☐ Issue Date	Notes	
Signer Signature		Witness Signature	

112 Service: ☐ Acknowledgment ☐ Oath/Affirmation ☐ Jurat ☐ Other/See Notes Fee $_____ Travel_____

Name (print)	Document type /Doc. name	Witness Name (print)	Date and Time Notarized _____ ___ ___ am / pm
Phone # / E-mail	Date of document	Witness Phone # / E-mail	Print of Right Thumb
Address	Satisfactory evidence of ID ☐ Driver's license ☐ Known Personally ☐ Credible Witness(es) ☐ Passport ☐ I.D. Card ☐ See Notes	Witness Address	
☐ ID. Issued by ☐ I.D. Number	☐ Expiration Date ☐ Issue Date	Notes	
Signer Signature		Witness Signature	

NOTARY PUBLIC JOURNAL – LARGE ENTRIES | 59

113 Service: ☐ Acknowledgment ☐ Oath/Affirmation ☐ Jurat ☐ Other/See Notes Fee $_____ Travel_____

Name (print)	Document type /Doc. name	Witness Name (print)	Date and Time Notarized _____ ___ _____ am / pm
Phone # / E-mail	Date of document	Witness Phone # / E-mail	Print of Right Thumb
Address	Satisfactory evidence of ID ☐ Driver's license ☐ Known Personally ☐ Credible Witness(es) ☐ Passport ☐ I.D. Card ☐ See Notes	Witness Address	
☐ ID. Issued by ☐ I.D. Number	☐ Expiration Date ☐ Issue Date	Notes	
Signer Signature		Witness Signature	

114 Service: ☐ Acknowledgment ☐ Oath/Affirmation ☐ Jurat ☐ Other/See Notes Fee $_____ Travel_____

Name (print)	Document type /Doc. name	Witness Name (print)	Date and Time Notarized _____ ___ _____ am / pm
Phone # / E-mail	Date of document	Witness Phone # / E-mail	Print of Right Thumb
Address	Satisfactory evidence of ID ☐ Driver's license ☐ Known Personally ☐ Credible Witness(es) ☐ Passport ☐ I.D. Card ☐ See Notes	Witness Address	
☐ ID. Issued by ☐ I.D. Number	☐ Expiration Date ☐ Issue Date	Notes	
Signer Signature		Witness Signature	

115

Service: ☐ Acknowledgment ☐ Oath/Affirmation ☐ Jurat ☐ Other/See Notes   Fee $_____   Travel_____

Name (print)	Document type /Doc. name	Witness Name (print)	Date and Time Notarized _____ ___ _____ am / pm
Phone # / E-mail	Date of document	Witness Phone # / E-mail	Print of Right Thumb
Address	Satisfactory evidence of ID ☐ Driver's license ☐ Known Personally ☐ Credible Witness(es) ☐ Passport ☐ I.D. Card ☐ See Notes	Witness Address	
☐ ID. Issued by ☐ I.D. Number	☐ Expiration Date ☐ Issue Date	Notes	
Signer Signature		Witness Signature	

116

Service: ☐ Acknowledgment ☐ Oath/Affirmation ☐ Jurat ☐ Other/See Notes   Fee $_____   Travel_____

Name (print)	Document type /Doc. name	Witness Name (print)	Date and Time Notarized _____ ___ _____ am / pm
Phone # / E-mail	Date of document	Witness Phone # / E-mail	Print of Right Thumb
Address	Satisfactory evidence of ID ☐ Driver's license ☐ Known Personally ☐ Credible Witness(es) ☐ Passport ☐ I.D. Card ☐ See Notes	Witness Address	
☐ ID. Issued by ☐ I.D. Number	☐ Expiration Date ☐ Issue Date	Notes	
Signer Signature		Witness Signature	

NOTARY PUBLIC JOURNAL – LARGE ENTRIES

117

Service: ☐ Acknowledgment ☐ Oath/Affirmation ☐ Jurat ☐ Other/See Notes Fee $_____ Travel_____				
Name (print)	Document type /Doc. name	Witness Name (print)	Date and Time Notarized _____ ___ _____ am / pm	
Phone # / E-mail	Date of document	Witness Phone # / E-mail	Print of Right Thumb	
Address	Satisfactory evidence of ID ☐ Driver's license ☐ Known Personally ☐ Credible Witness(es) ☐ Passport ☐ I.D. Card ☐ See Notes	Witness Address		
☐ ID. Issued by	☐ Expiration Date	Notes		
☐ I.D. Number	☐ Issue Date			
Signer Signature		Witness Signature		

118

Service: ☐ Acknowledgment ☐ Oath/Affirmation ☐ Jurat ☐ Other/See Notes Fee $_____ Travel_____				
Name (print)	Document type /Doc. name	Witness Name (print)	Date and Time Notarized _____ ___ _____ am / pm	
Phone # / E-mail	Date of document	Witness Phone # / E-mail	Print of Right Thumb	
Address	Satisfactory evidence of ID ☐ Driver's license ☐ Known Personally ☐ Credible Witness(es) ☐ Passport ☐ I.D. Card ☐ See Notes	Witness Address		
☐ ID. Issued by	☐ Expiration Date	Notes		
☐ I.D. Number	☐ Issue Date			
Signer Signature		Witness Signature		

119

Service: ☐ Acknowledgment ☐ Oath/Affirmation ☐ Jurat ☐ Other/See Notes Fee $_____ Travel_____

Name (print)	Document type /Doc. name	Witness Name (print)	Date and Time Notarized _____ ____ ____ am / pm
Phone # / E-mail	Date of document	Witness Phone # / E-mail	Print of Right Thumb
Address	Satisfactory evidence of ID ☐ Driver's license ☐ Known Personally ☐ Credible Witness(es) ☐ Passport ☐ I.D. Card ☐ See Notes	Witness Address	
☐ ID. Issued by ☐ I.D. Number	☐ Expiration Date ☐ Issue Date	Notes	
Signer Signature		Witness Signature	

120

Service: ☐ Acknowledgment ☐ Oath/Affirmation ☐ Jurat ☐ Other/See Notes Fee $_____ Travel_____

Name (print)	Document type /Doc. name	Witness Name (print)	Date and Time Notarized _____ ____ ____ am / pm
Phone # / E-mail	Date of document	Witness Phone # / E-mail	Print of Right Thumb
Address	Satisfactory evidence of ID ☐ Driver's license ☐ Known Personally ☐ Credible Witness(es) ☐ Passport ☐ I.D. Card ☐ See Notes	Witness Address	
☐ ID. Issued by ☐ I.D. Number	☐ Expiration Date ☐ Issue Date	Notes	
Signer Signature		Witness Signature	

121

Service: ☐ Acknowledgment ☐ Oath/Affirmation ☐ Jurat ☐ Other/See Notes Fee $_____ Travel_____

Name (print)	Document type /Doc. name	Witness Name (print)	Date and Time Notarized _____ ___ ___ am / pm
Phone # / E-mail	Date of document	Witness Phone # / E-mail	Print of Right Thumb
Address	Satisfactory evidence of ID ☐ Driver's license ☐ Known Personally ☐ Credible Witness(es) ☐ Passport ☐ I.D. Card ☐ See Notes	Witness Address	
☐ ID. Issued by	☐ Expiration Date	Notes	
☐ I.D. Number	☐ Issue Date		
Signer Signature		Witness Signature	

122

Service: ☐ Acknowledgment ☐ Oath/Affirmation ☐ Jurat ☐ Other/See Notes Fee $_____ Travel_____

Name (print)	Document type /Doc. name	Witness Name (print)	Date and Time Notarized _____ ___ ___ am / pm
Phone # / E-mail	Date of document	Witness Phone # / E-mail	Print of Right Thumb
Address	Satisfactory evidence of ID ☐ Driver's license ☐ Known Personally ☐ Credible Witness(es) ☐ Passport ☐ I.D. Card ☐ See Notes	Witness Address	
☐ ID. Issued by	☐ Expiration Date	Notes	
☐ I.D. Number	☐ Issue Date		
Signer Signature		Witness Signature	

NOTARY PUBLIC JOURNAL – LARGE ENTRIES

123

Service: ☐ Acknowledgment ☐ Oath/Affirmation ☐ Jurat ☐ Other/See Notes Fee $_____ Travel_____

Name (print)	Document type /Doc. name	Witness Name (print)	Date and Time Notarized _____ ___ _____ am / pm
Phone # / E-mail	Date of document	Witness Phone # / E-mail	Print of Right Thumb
Address	Satisfactory evidence of ID ☐ Driver's license ☐ Known Personally ☐ Credible Witness(es) ☐ Passport ☐ I.D. Card ☐ See Notes	Witness Address	
☐ ID. Issued by ☐ I.D. Number	☐ Expiration Date ☐ Issue Date	Notes	
Signer Signature		Witness Signature	

124

Service: ☐ Acknowledgment ☐ Oath/Affirmation ☐ Jurat ☐ Other/See Notes Fee $_____ Travel_____

Name (print)	Document type /Doc. name	Witness Name (print)	Date and Time Notarized _____ ___ _____ am / pm
Phone # / E-mail	Date of document	Witness Phone # / E-mail	Print of Right Thumb
Address	Satisfactory evidence of ID ☐ Driver's license ☐ Known Personally ☐ Credible Witness(es) ☐ Passport ☐ I.D. Card ☐ See Notes	Witness Address	
☐ ID. Issued by ☐ I.D. Number	☐ Expiration Date ☐ Issue Date	Notes	
Signer Signature		Witness Signature	

NOTARY PUBLIC JOURNAL – LARGE ENTRIES | 65

125 Service: ☐ Acknowledgment ☐ Oath/Affirmation ☐ Jurat ☐ Other/See Notes Fee $_____ Travel_____

Name (print)	Document type /Doc. name	Witness Name (print)	Date and Time Notarized _____ ____ _____ am / pm
Phone # / E-mail	Date of document	Witness Phone # / E-mail	Print of Right Thumb
Address	Satisfactory evidence of ID ☐ Driver's license ☐ Known Personally ☐ Credible Witness(es) ☐ Passport ☐ I.D. Card ☐ See Notes	Witness Address	
☐ ID. Issued by ☐ I.D. Number	☐ Expiration Date ☐ Issue Date	Notes	
Signer Signature		Witness Signature	

126 Service: ☐ Acknowledgment ☐ Oath/Affirmation ☐ Jurat ☐ Other/See Notes Fee $_____ Travel_____

Name (print)	Document type /Doc. name	Witness Name (print)	Date and Time Notarized _____ ____ _____ am / pm
Phone # / E-mail	Date of document	Witness Phone # / E-mail	Print of Right Thumb
Address	Satisfactory evidence of ID ☐ Driver's license ☐ Known Personally ☐ Credible Witness(es) ☐ Passport ☐ I.D. Card ☐ See Notes	Witness Address	
☐ ID. Issued by ☐ I.D. Number	☐ Expiration Date ☐ Issue Date	Notes	
Signer Signature		Witness Signature	

127

Service: ☐ Acknowledgment ☐ Oath/Affirmation ☐ Jurat ☐ Other/See Notes   Fee $_____   Travel_____

Name (print)	Document type /Doc. name	Witness Name (print)	Date and Time Notarized
			_____ ___ ___ am / pm
Phone # / E-mail	Date of document	Witness Phone # / E-mail	Print of Right Thumb
Address	Satisfactory evidence of ID ☐ Driver's license ☐ Known Personally ☐ Credible Witness(es) ☐ Passport ☐ I.D. Card ☐ See Notes	Witness Address	
☐ ID. Issued by ☐ I.D. Number	☐ Expiration Date ☐ Issue Date	Notes	
Signer Signature		Witness Signature	

128

Service: ☐ Acknowledgment ☐ Oath/Affirmation ☐ Jurat ☐ Other/See Notes   Fee $_____   Travel_____

Name (print)	Document type /Doc. name	Witness Name (print)	Date and Time Notarized
			_____ ___ ___ am / pm
Phone # / E-mail	Date of document	Witness Phone # / E-mail	Print of Right Thumb
Address	Satisfactory evidence of ID ☐ Driver's license ☐ Known Personally ☐ Credible Witness(es) ☐ Passport ☐ I.D. Card ☐ See Notes	Witness Address	
☐ ID. Issued by ☐ I.D. Number	☐ Expiration Date ☐ Issue Date	Notes	
Signer Signature		Witness Signature	

129

Service: ☐ Acknowledgment ☐ Oath/Affirmation ☐ Jurat ☐ Other/See Notes   Fee $_____   Travel_____

Name (print)	Document type /Doc. name	Witness Name (print)	Date and Time Notarized _____ ___ _____ am / pm
Phone # / E-mail	Date of document	Witness Phone # / E-mail	Print of Right Thumb
Address	Satisfactory evidence of ID ☐ Driver's license ☐ Known Personally ☐ Credible Witness(es) ☐ Passport ☐ I.D. Card ☐ See Notes	Witness Address	
☐ ID. Issued by ☐ I.D. Number	☐ Expiration Date ☐ Issue Date	Notes	
Signer Signature		Witness Signature	

130

Service: ☐ Acknowledgment ☐ Oath/Affirmation ☐ Jurat ☐ Other/See Notes   Fee $_____   Travel_____

Name (print)	Document type /Doc. name	Witness Name (print)	Date and Time Notarized _____ ___ _____ am / pm
Phone # / E-mail	Date of document	Witness Phone # / E-mail	Print of Right Thumb
Address	Satisfactory evidence of ID ☐ Driver's license ☐ Known Personally ☐ Credible Witness(es) ☐ Passport ☐ I.D. Card ☐ See Notes	Witness Address	
☐ ID. Issued by ☐ I.D. Number	☐ Expiration Date ☐ Issue Date	Notes	
Signer Signature		Witness Signature	

68 | NOTARY PUBLIC JOURNAL – LARGE ENTRIES

131 Service: ☐ Acknowledgment ☐ Oath/Affirmation ☐ Jurat ☐ Other/See Notes Fee $_____ Travel_____

Name (print)	Document type /Doc. name	Witness Name (print)	Date and Time Notarized
			_____ ___ _____ am / pm
Phone # / E-mail	Date of document	Witness Phone # / E-mail	Print of Right Thumb
Address	Satisfactory evidence of ID ☐ Driver's license ☐ Known Personally ☐ Credible Witness(es) ☐ Passport ☐ I.D. Card ☐ See Notes	Witness Address	
☐ ID. Issued by ☐ I.D. Number	☐ Expiration Date ☐ Issue Date	Notes	
Signer Signature		Witness Signature	

132 Service: ☐ Acknowledgment ☐ Oath/Affirmation ☐ Jurat ☐ Other/See Notes Fee $_____ Travel_____

Name (print)	Document type /Doc. name	Witness Name (print)	Date and Time Notarized
			_____ ___ _____ am / pm
Phone # / E-mail	Date of document	Witness Phone # / E-mail	Print of Right Thumb
Address	Satisfactory evidence of ID ☐ Driver's license ☐ Known Personally ☐ Credible Witness(es) ☐ Passport ☐ I.D. Card ☐ See Notes	Witness Address	
☐ ID. Issued by ☐ I.D. Number	☐ Expiration Date ☐ Issue Date	Notes	
Signer Signature		Witness Signature	

NOTARY PUBLIC JOURNAL – LARGE ENTRIES

133 | Service: ☐ Acknowledgment ☐ Oath/Affirmation ☐ Jurat ☐ Other/See Notes Fee $_____ Travel_____

Name (print)	Document type /Doc. name	Witness Name (print)	Date and Time Notarized _____ ___ _____ am / pm
Phone # / E-mail	Date of document	Witness Phone # / E-mail	Print of Right Thumb
Address	Satisfactory evidence of ID ☐ Driver's license ☐ Known Personally ☐ Credible Witness(es) ☐ Passport ☐ I.D. Card ☐ See Notes	Witness Address	
☐ ID. Issued by ☐ I.D. Number	☐ Expiration Date ☐ Issue Date	Notes	
Signer Signature		Witness Signature	

134 | Service: ☐ Acknowledgment ☐ Oath/Affirmation ☐ Jurat ☐ Other/See Notes Fee $_____ Travel_____

Name (print)	Document type /Doc. name	Witness Name (print)	Date and Time Notarized _____ ___ _____ am / pm
Phone # / E-mail	Date of document	Witness Phone # / E-mail	Print of Right Thumb
Address	Satisfactory evidence of ID ☐ Driver's license ☐ Known Personally ☐ Credible Witness(es) ☐ Passport ☐ I.D. Card ☐ See Notes	Witness Address	
☐ ID. Issued by ☐ I.D. Number	☐ Expiration Date ☐ Issue Date	Notes	
Signer Signature		Witness Signature	

NOTARY PUBLIC JOURNAL – LARGE ENTRIES

135
Service: ☐ Acknowledgment ☐ Oath/Affirmation ☐ Jurat ☐ Other/See Notes Fee $_____ Travel_____

Name (print)	Document type /Doc. name	Witness Name (print)	Date and Time Notarized _____ ___ ___ am / pm
Phone # / E-mail	Date of document	Witness Phone # / E-mail	Print of Right Thumb
Address	Satisfactory evidence of ID ☐ Driver's license ☐ Known Personally ☐ Credible Witness(es) ☐ Passport ☐ I.D. Card ☐ See Notes	Witness Address	
☐ ID. Issued by ☐ I.D. Number	☐ Expiration Date ☐ Issue Date	Notes	
Signer Signature		Witness Signature	

136
Service: ☐ Acknowledgment ☐ Oath/Affirmation ☐ Jurat ☐ Other/See Notes Fee $_____ Travel_____

Name (print)	Document type /Doc. name	Witness Name (print)	Date and Time Notarized _____ ___ ___ am / pm
Phone # / E-mail	Date of document	Witness Phone # / E-mail	Print of Right Thumb
Address	Satisfactory evidence of ID ☐ Driver's license ☐ Known Personally ☐ Credible Witness(es) ☐ Passport ☐ I.D. Card ☐ See Notes	Witness Address	
☐ ID. Issued by ☐ I.D. Number	☐ Expiration Date ☐ Issue Date	Notes	
Signer Signature		Witness Signature	

NOTARY PUBLIC JOURNAL – LARGE ENTRIES | 71

137 Service: ☐ Acknowledgment ☐ Oath/Affirmation ☐ Jurat ☐ Other/See Notes Fee $_____ Travel_____

Name (print)	Document type /Doc. name	Witness Name (print)	Date and Time Notarized _____ ___ _____ am / pm
Phone # / E-mail	Date of document	Witness Phone # / E-mail	Print of Right Thumb
Address	Satisfactory evidence of ID ☐ Driver's license ☐ Known Personally ☐ Credible Witness(es) ☐ Passport ☐ I.D. Card ☐ See Notes	Witness Address	
☐ ID. Issued by ☐ I.D. Number	☐ Expiration Date ☐ Issue Date	Notes	
Signer Signature		Witness Signature	

138 Service: ☐ Acknowledgment ☐ Oath/Affirmation ☐ Jurat ☐ Other/See Notes Fee $_____ Travel_____

Name (print)	Document type /Doc. name	Witness Name (print)	Date and Time Notarized _____ ___ _____ am / pm
Phone # / E-mail	Date of document	Witness Phone # / E-mail	Print of Right Thumb
Address	Satisfactory evidence of ID ☐ Driver's license ☐ Known Personally ☐ Credible Witness(es) ☐ Passport ☐ I.D. Card ☐ See Notes	Witness Address	
☐ ID. Issued by ☐ I.D. Number	☐ Expiration Date ☐ Issue Date	Notes	
Signer Signature		Witness Signature	

NOTARY PUBLIC JOURNAL – LARGE ENTRIES

139
Service: ☐ Acknowledgment ☐ Oath/Affirmation ☐ Jurat ☐ Other/See Notes   Fee $_____   Travel_____

Name (print)	Document type /Doc. name	Witness Name (print)	Date and Time Notarized
			_____ ____ ____ am / pm
Phone # / E-mail	Date of document	Witness Phone # / E-mail	Print of Right Thumb
Address	Satisfactory evidence of ID ☐ Driver's license ☐ Known Personally ☐ Credible Witness(es) ☐ Passport ☐ I.D. Card ☐ See Notes	Witness Address	
☐ ID. Issued by	☐ Expiration Date	Notes	
☐ I.D. Number	☐ Issue Date		
Signer Signature		Witness Signature	

140
Service: ☐ Acknowledgment ☐ Oath/Affirmation ☐ Jurat ☐ Other/See Notes   Fee $_____   Travel_____

Name (print)	Document type /Doc. name	Witness Name (print)	Date and Time Notarized
			_____ ____ ____ am / pm
Phone # / E-mail	Date of document	Witness Phone # / E-mail	Print of Right Thumb
Address	Satisfactory evidence of ID ☐ Driver's license ☐ Known Personally ☐ Credible Witness(es) ☐ Passport ☐ I.D. Card ☐ See Notes	Witness Address	
☐ ID. Issued by	☐ Expiration Date	Notes	
☐ I.D. Number	☐ Issue Date		
Signer Signature		Witness Signature	

141

Service: ☐ Acknowledgment ☐ Oath/Affirmation ☐ Jurat ☐ Other/See Notes Fee $_____ Travel_____

Name (print)	Document type /Doc. name	Witness Name (print)	Date and Time Notarized _____ ___ _____ am / pm
Phone # / E-mail	Date of document	Witness Phone # / E-mail	Print of Right Thumb
Address	Satisfactory evidence of ID ☐ Driver's license ☐ Known Personally ☐ Credible Witness(es) ☐ Passport ☐ I.D. Card ☐ See Notes	Witness Address	
☐ ID. Issued by ☐ I.D. Number	☐ Expiration Date ☐ Issue Date	Notes	
Signer Signature		Witness Signature	

142

Service: ☐ Acknowledgment ☐ Oath/Affirmation ☐ Jurat ☐ Other/See Notes Fee $_____ Travel_____

Name (print)	Document type /Doc. name	Witness Name (print)	Date and Time Notarized _____ ___ _____ am / pm
Phone # / E-mail	Date of document	Witness Phone # / E-mail	Print of Right Thumb
Address	Satisfactory evidence of ID ☐ Driver's license ☐ Known Personally ☐ Credible Witness(es) ☐ Passport ☐ I.D. Card ☐ See Notes	Witness Address	
☐ ID. Issued by ☐ I.D. Number	☐ Expiration Date ☐ Issue Date	Notes	
Signer Signature		Witness Signature	

143 Service: ☐ Acknowledgment ☐ Oath/Affirmation ☐ Jurat ☐ Other/See Notes Fee $_____ Travel_____

Name (print)	Document type /Doc. name	Witness Name (print)	Date and Time Notarized _____ ___ ___ am / pm
Phone # / E-mail	Date of document	Witness Phone # / E-mail	Print of Right Thumb
Address	Satisfactory evidence of ID ☐ Driver's license ☐ Known Personally ☐ Credible Witness(es) ☐ Passport ☐ I.D. Card ☐ See Notes	Witness Address	
☐ ID. Issued by ☐ I.D. Number	☐ Expiration Date ☐ Issue Date	Notes	
Signer Signature		Witness Signature	

144 Service: ☐ Acknowledgment ☐ Oath/Affirmation ☐ Jurat ☐ Other/See Notes Fee $_____ Travel_____

Name (print)	Document type /Doc. name	Witness Name (print)	Date and Time Notarized _____ ___ ___ am / pm
Phone # / E-mail	Date of document	Witness Phone # / E-mail	Print of Right Thumb
Address	Satisfactory evidence of ID ☐ Driver's license ☐ Known Personally ☐ Credible Witness(es) ☐ Passport ☐ I.D. Card ☐ See Notes	Witness Address	
☐ ID. Issued by ☐ I.D. Number	☐ Expiration Date ☐ Issue Date	Notes	
Signer Signature		Witness Signature	

NOTARY PUBLIC JOURNAL – LARGE ENTRIES | 75

145 | Service: ☐ Acknowledgment ☐ Oath/Affirmation ☐ Jurat ☐ Other/See Notes Fee $_____ Travel_____

Name (print)	Document type /Doc. name	Witness Name (print)	Date and Time Notarized _____ ___ _____ am / pm
Phone # / E-mail	Date of document	Witness Phone # / E-mail	Print of Right Thumb
Address	Satisfactory evidence of ID ☐ Driver's license ☐ Known Personally ☐ Credible Witness(es) ☐ Passport ☐ I.D. Card ☐ See Notes	Witness Address	
☐ ID. Issued by ☐ I.D. Number	☐ Expiration Date ☐ Issue Date	Notes	
Signer Signature		Witness Signature	

146 | Service: ☐ Acknowledgment ☐ Oath/Affirmation ☐ Jurat ☐ Other/See Notes Fee $_____ Travel_____

Name (print)	Document type /Doc. name	Witness Name (print)	Date and Time Notarized _____ ___ _____ am / pm
Phone # / E-mail	Date of document	Witness Phone # / E-mail	Print of Right Thumb
Address	Satisfactory evidence of ID ☐ Driver's license ☐ Known Personally ☐ Credible Witness(es) ☐ Passport ☐ I.D. Card ☐ See Notes	Witness Address	
☐ ID. Issued by ☐ I.D. Number	☐ Expiration Date ☐ Issue Date	Notes	
Signer Signature		Witness Signature	

147

Service: ☐ Acknowledgment ☐ Oath/Affirmation ☐ Jurat ☐ Other/See Notes Fee $_____ Travel_____

Name (print)	Document type /Doc. name	Witness Name (print)	Date and Time Notarized _____ ____ ____ am / pm
Phone # / E-mail	Date of document	Witness Phone # / E-mail	Print of Right Thumb
Address	Satisfactory evidence of ID ☐ Driver's license ☐ Known Personally ☐ Credible Witness(es) ☐ Passport ☐ I.D. Card ☐ See Notes	Witness Address	
☐ ID. Issued by ☐ I.D. Number	☐ Expiration Date ☐ Issue Date	Notes	
Signer Signature		Witness Signature	

148

Service: ☐ Acknowledgment ☐ Oath/Affirmation ☐ Jurat ☐ Other/See Notes Fee $_____ Travel_____

Name (print)	Document type /Doc. name	Witness Name (print)	Date and Time Notarized _____ ____ ____ am / pm
Phone # / E-mail	Date of document	Witness Phone # / E-mail	Print of Right Thumb
Address	Satisfactory evidence of ID ☐ Driver's license ☐ Known Personally ☐ Credible Witness(es) ☐ Passport ☐ I.D. Card ☐ See Notes	Witness Address	
☐ ID. Issued by ☐ I.D. Number	☐ Expiration Date ☐ Issue Date	Notes	
Signer Signature		Witness Signature	

NOTARY PUBLIC JOURNAL – LARGE ENTRIES

149

Service: ☐ Acknowledgment ☐ Oath/Affirmation ☐ Jurat ☐ Other/See Notes   Fee $_____   Travel_____

Name (print)	Document type /Doc. name	Witness Name (print)	Date and Time Notarized _____ ___ _____ am / pm
Phone # / E-mail	Date of document	Witness Phone # / E-mail	Print of Right Thumb
Address	Satisfactory evidence of ID ☐ Driver's license ☐ Known Personally ☐ Credible Witness(es) ☐ Passport ☐ I.D. Card ☐ See Notes	Witness Address	
☐ ID. Issued by	☐ Expiration Date	Notes	
☐ I.D. Number	☐ Issue Date		
Signer Signature		Witness Signature	

150

Service: ☐ Acknowledgment ☐ Oath/Affirmation ☐ Jurat ☐ Other/See Notes   Fee $_____   Travel_____

Name (print)	Document type /Doc. name	Witness Name (print)	Date and Time Notarized _____ ___ _____ am / pm
Phone # / E-mail	Date of document	Witness Phone # / E-mail	Print of Right Thumb
Address	Satisfactory evidence of ID ☐ Driver's license ☐ Known Personally ☐ Credible Witness(es) ☐ Passport ☐ I.D. Card ☐ See Notes	Witness Address	
☐ ID. Issued by	☐ Expiration Date	Notes	
☐ I.D. Number	☐ Issue Date		
Signer Signature		Witness Signature	

78 NOTARY PUBLIC JOURNAL – LARGE ENTRIES

151
Service: ☐ Acknowledgment ☐ Oath/Affirmation ☐ Jurat ☐ Other/See Notes Fee $_____ Travel_____

Name (print)	Document type /Doc. name	Witness Name (print)	Date and Time Notarized _____ ___ ___ am / pm
Phone # / E-mail	Date of document	Witness Phone # / E-mail	Print of Right Thumb
Address	Satisfactory evidence of ID ☐ Driver's license ☐ Known Personally ☐ Credible Witness(es) ☐ Passport ☐ I.D. Card ☐ See Notes	Witness Address	
☐ ID. Issued by ☐ I.D. Number	☐ Expiration Date ☐ Issue Date	Notes	
Signer Signature		Witness Signature	

152
Service: ☐ Acknowledgment ☐ Oath/Affirmation ☐ Jurat ☐ Other/See Notes Fee $_____ Travel_____

Name (print)	Document type /Doc. name	Witness Name (print)	Date and Time Notarized _____ ___ ___ am / pm
Phone # / E-mail	Date of document	Witness Phone # / E-mail	Print of Right Thumb
Address	Satisfactory evidence of ID ☐ Driver's license ☐ Known Personally ☐ Credible Witness(es) ☐ Passport ☐ I.D. Card ☐ See Notes	Witness Address	
☐ ID. Issued by ☐ I.D. Number	☐ Expiration Date ☐ Issue Date	Notes	
Signer Signature		Witness Signature	

153 Service: ☐ Acknowledgment ☐ Oath/Affirmation ☐ Jurat ☐ Other/See Notes Fee $_____ Travel_____

Name (print)	Document type /Doc. name	Witness Name (print)	Date and Time Notarized _____ ___ _____ am / pm
Phone # / E-mail	Date of document	Witness Phone # / E-mail	Print of Right Thumb
Address	Satisfactory evidence of ID ☐ Driver's license ☐ Known Personally ☐ Credible Witness(es) ☐ Passport ☐ I.D. Card ☐ See Notes	Witness Address	
☐ ID. Issued by ☐ I.D. Number	☐ Expiration Date ☐ Issue Date	Notes	
Signer Signature		Witness Signature	

154 Service: ☐ Acknowledgment ☐ Oath/Affirmation ☐ Jurat ☐ Other/See Notes Fee $_____ Travel_____

Name (print)	Document type /Doc. name	Witness Name (print)	Date and Time Notarized _____ ___ _____ am / pm
Phone # / E-mail	Date of document	Witness Phone # / E-mail	Print of Right Thumb
Address	Satisfactory evidence of ID ☐ Driver's license ☐ Known Personally ☐ Credible Witness(es) ☐ Passport ☐ I.D. Card ☐ See Notes	Witness Address	
☐ ID. Issued by ☐ I.D. Number	☐ Expiration Date ☐ Issue Date	Notes	
Signer Signature		Witness Signature	

NOTARY PUBLIC JOURNAL – LARGE ENTRIES

155
Service: ☐ Acknowledgment ☐ Oath/Affirmation ☐ Jurat ☐ Other/See Notes   Fee $_____   Travel_____

Name (print)	Document type /Doc. name	Witness Name (print)	Date and Time Notarized _____ ___ _____ am / pm
Phone # / E-mail	Date of document	Witness Phone # / E-mail	Print of Right Thumb
Address	Satisfactory evidence of ID ☐ Driver's license ☐ Known Personally ☐ Credible Witness(es) ☐ Passport ☐ I.D. Card ☐ See Notes	Witness Address	
☐ ID. Issued by ☐ I.D. Number	☐ Expiration Date ☐ Issue Date	Notes	
Signer Signature		Witness Signature	

156
Service: ☐ Acknowledgment ☐ Oath/Affirmation ☐ Jurat ☐ Other/See Notes   Fee $_____   Travel_____

Name (print)	Document type /Doc. name	Witness Name (print)	Date and Time Notarized _____ ___ _____ am / pm
Phone # / E-mail	Date of document	Witness Phone # / E-mail	Print of Right Thumb
Address	Satisfactory evidence of ID ☐ Driver's license ☐ Known Personally ☐ Credible Witness(es) ☐ Passport ☐ I.D. Card ☐ See Notes	Witness Address	
☐ ID. Issued by ☐ I.D. Number	☐ Expiration Date ☐ Issue Date	Notes	
Signer Signature		Witness Signature	

NOTARY PUBLIC JOURNAL – LARGE ENTRIES

157
Service: ☐ Acknowledgment ☐ Oath/Affirmation ☐ Jurat ☐ Other/See Notes   Fee $_____   Travel_____

Name (print)	Document type /Doc. name	Witness Name (print)	Date and Time Notarized _____ ___ _____ am / pm
Phone # / E-mail	Date of document	Witness Phone # / E-mail	Print of Right Thumb
Address	Satisfactory evidence of ID ☐ Driver's license ☐ Known Personally ☐ Credible Witness(es) ☐ Passport ☐ I.D. Card ☐ See Notes	Witness Address	
☐ ID. Issued by ☐ I.D. Number	☐ Expiration Date ☐ Issue Date	Notes	
Signer Signature		Witness Signature	

158
Service: ☐ Acknowledgment ☐ Oath/Affirmation ☐ Jurat ☐ Other/See Notes   Fee $_____   Travel_____

Name (print)	Document type /Doc. name	Witness Name (print)	Date and Time Notarized _____ ___ _____ am / pm
Phone # / E-mail	Date of document	Witness Phone # / E-mail	Print of Right Thumb
Address	Satisfactory evidence of ID ☐ Driver's license ☐ Known Personally ☐ Credible Witness(es) ☐ Passport ☐ I.D. Card ☐ See Notes	Witness Address	
☐ ID. Issued by ☐ I.D. Number	☐ Expiration Date ☐ Issue Date	Notes	
Signer Signature		Witness Signature	

NOTARY PUBLIC JOURNAL – LARGE ENTRIES

159
Service: ☐ Acknowledgment ☐ Oath/Affirmation ☐ Jurat ☐ Other/See Notes   Fee $_____   Travel_____

Name (print)	Document type /Doc. name	Witness Name (print)	Date and Time Notarized _____ ___ ___ am / pm
Phone # / E-mail	Date of document	Witness Phone # / E-mail	Print of Right Thumb
Address	Satisfactory evidence of ID ☐ Driver's license ☐ Known Personally ☐ Credible Witness(es) ☐ Passport ☐ I.D. Card ☐ See Notes	Witness Address	
☐ ID. Issued by ☐ I.D. Number	☐ Expiration Date ☐ Issue Date	Notes	
Signer Signature		Witness Signature	

160
Service: ☐ Acknowledgment ☐ Oath/Affirmation ☐ Jurat ☐ Other/See Notes   Fee $_____   Travel_____

Name (print)	Document type /Doc. name	Witness Name (print)	Date and Time Notarized _____ ___ ___ am / pm
Phone # / E-mail	Date of document	Witness Phone # / E-mail	Print of Right Thumb
Address	Satisfactory evidence of ID ☐ Driver's license ☐ Known Personally ☐ Credible Witness(es) ☐ Passport ☐ I.D. Card ☐ See Notes	Witness Address	
☐ ID. Issued by ☐ I.D. Number	☐ Expiration Date ☐ Issue Date	Notes	
Signer Signature		Witness Signature	

NOTARY PUBLIC JOURNAL – LARGE ENTRIES | 83

161

Service: ☐ Acknowledgment ☐ Oath/Affirmation ☐ Jurat ☐ Other/See Notes Fee $_____ Travel_____				
Name (print)	Document type /Doc. name	Witness Name (print)	Date and Time Notarized _____ ____ _____ am / pm	
Phone # / E-mail	Date of document	Witness Phone # / E-mail	Print of Right Thumb	
Address	Satisfactory evidence of ID ☐ Driver's license ☐ Known Personally ☐ Credible Witness(es) ☐ Passport ☐ I.D. Card ☐ See Notes	Witness Address		
☐ ID. Issued by	☐ Expiration Date	Notes		
☐ I.D. Number	☐ Issue Date			
Signer Signature		Witness Signature		

162

Service: ☐ Acknowledgment ☐ Oath/Affirmation ☐ Jurat ☐ Other/See Notes Fee $_____ Travel_____				
Name (print)	Document type /Doc. name	Witness Name (print)	Date and Time Notarized _____ ____ _____ am / pm	
Phone # / E-mail	Date of document	Witness Phone # / E-mail	Print of Right Thumb	
Address	Satisfactory evidence of ID ☐ Driver's license ☐ Known Personally ☐ Credible Witness(es) ☐ Passport ☐ I.D. Card ☐ See Notes	Witness Address		
☐ ID. Issued by	☐ Expiration Date	Notes		
☐ I.D. Number	☐ Issue Date			
Signer Signature		Witness Signature		

84 | NOTARY PUBLIC JOURNAL – LARGE ENTRIES

163 Service: ☐ Acknowledgment ☐ Oath/Affirmation ☐ Jurat ☐ Other/See Notes Fee $_____ Travel_____

Name (print)	Document type /Doc. name	Witness Name (print)	Date and Time Notarized _____ ___ _____ am / pm
Phone # / E-mail	Date of document	Witness Phone # / E-mail	Print of Right Thumb
Address	Satisfactory evidence of ID ☐ Driver's license ☐ Known Personally ☐ Credible Witness(es) ☐ Passport ☐ I.D. Card ☐ See Notes	Witness Address	
☐ ID. Issued by ☐ I.D. Number	☐ Expiration Date ☐ Issue Date	Notes	
Signer Signature		Witness Signature	

164 Service: ☐ Acknowledgment ☐ Oath/Affirmation ☐ Jurat ☐ Other/See Notes Fee $_____ Travel_____

Name (print)	Document type /Doc. name	Witness Name (print)	Date and Time Notarized _____ ___ _____ am / pm
Phone # / E-mail	Date of document	Witness Phone # / E-mail	Print of Right Thumb
Address	Satisfactory evidence of ID ☐ Driver's license ☐ Known Personally ☐ Credible Witness(es) ☐ Passport ☐ I.D. Card ☐ See Notes	Witness Address	
☐ ID. Issued by ☐ I.D. Number	☐ Expiration Date ☐ Issue Date	Notes	
Signer Signature		Witness Signature	

NOTARY PUBLIC JOURNAL – LARGE ENTRIES | 85

165 Service: ☐ Acknowledgment ☐ Oath/Affirmation ☐ Jurat ☐ Other/See Notes Fee $_____ Travel_____

Name (print)	Document type /Doc. name	Witness Name (print)	Date and Time Notarized
			_____ ___ _____ am / pm
Phone # / E-mail	Date of document	Witness Phone # / E-mail	Print of Right Thumb
Address	Satisfactory evidence of ID ☐ Driver's license ☐ Known Personally ☐ Credible Witness(es) ☐ Passport ☐ I.D. Card ☐ See Notes	Witness Address	
☐ ID. Issued by	☐ Expiration Date	Notes	
☐ I.D. Number	☐ Issue Date		
Signer Signature		Witness Signature	

166 Service: ☐ Acknowledgment ☐ Oath/Affirmation ☐ Jurat ☐ Other/See Notes Fee $_____ Travel_____

Name (print)	Document type /Doc. name	Witness Name (print)	Date and Time Notarized
			_____ ___ _____ am / pm
Phone # / E-mail	Date of document	Witness Phone # / E-mail	Print of Right Thumb
Address	Satisfactory evidence of ID ☐ Driver's license ☐ Known Personally ☐ Credible Witness(es) ☐ Passport ☐ I.D. Card ☐ See Notes	Witness Address	
☐ ID. Issued by	☐ Expiration Date	Notes	
☐ I.D. Number	☐ Issue Date		
Signer Signature		Witness Signature	

86 | NOTARY PUBLIC JOURNAL – LARGE ENTRIES

167 Service: ☐ Acknowledgment ☐ Oath/Affirmation ☐ Jurat ☐ Other/See Notes   Fee $_____   Travel_____

Name (print)	Document type /Doc. name	Witness Name (print)	Date and Time Notarized _____ ___ _____ am / pm
Phone # / E-mail	Date of document	Witness Phone # / E-mail	Print of Right Thumb
Address	Satisfactory evidence of ID ☐ Driver's license ☐ Known Personally ☐ Credible Witness(es) ☐ Passport ☐ I.D. Card ☐ See Notes	Witness Address	
☐ ID. Issued by ☐ I.D. Number	☐ Expiration Date ☐ Issue Date	Notes	
Signer Signature		Witness Signature	

168 Service: ☐ Acknowledgment ☐ Oath/Affirmation ☐ Jurat ☐ Other/See Notes   Fee $_____   Travel_____

Name (print)	Document type /Doc. name	Witness Name (print)	Date and Time Notarized _____ ___ _____ am / pm
Phone # / E-mail	Date of document	Witness Phone # / E-mail	Print of Right Thumb
Address	Satisfactory evidence of ID ☐ Driver's license ☐ Known Personally ☐ Credible Witness(es) ☐ Passport ☐ I.D. Card ☐ See Notes	Witness Address	
☐ ID. Issued by ☐ I.D. Number	☐ Expiration Date ☐ Issue Date	Notes	
Signer Signature		Witness Signature	

NOTARY PUBLIC JOURNAL – LARGE ENTRIES | 87

169 Service: ☐ Acknowledgment ☐ Oath/Affirmation ☐ Jurat ☐ Other/See Notes   Fee $_____   Travel_____

Name (print)	Document type /Doc. name	Witness Name (print)	Date and Time Notarized _____ ___ _____ am / pm
Phone # / E-mail	Date of document	Witness Phone # / E-mail	Print of Right Thumb
Address	Satisfactory evidence of ID ☐ Driver's license ☐ Known Personally ☐ Credible Witness(es) ☐ Passport ☐ I.D. Card ☐ See Notes	Witness Address	
☐ ID. Issued by	☐ Expiration Date	Notes	
☐ I.D. Number	☐ Issue Date		
Signer Signature		Witness Signature	

170 Service: ☐ Acknowledgment ☐ Oath/Affirmation ☐ Jurat ☐ Other/See Notes   Fee $_____   Travel_____

Name (print)	Document type /Doc. name	Witness Name (print)	Date and Time Notarized _____ ___ _____ am / pm
Phone # / E-mail	Date of document	Witness Phone # / E-mail	Print of Right Thumb
Address	Satisfactory evidence of ID ☐ Driver's license ☐ Known Personally ☐ Credible Witness(es) ☐ Passport ☐ I.D. Card ☐ See Notes	Witness Address	
☐ ID. Issued by	☐ Expiration Date	Notes	
☐ I.D. Number	☐ Issue Date		
Signer Signature		Witness Signature	

88 | NOTARY PUBLIC JOURNAL – LARGE ENTRIES

171
Service: ☐ Acknowledgment ☐ Oath/Affirmation ☐ Jurat ☐ Other/See Notes Fee $_____ Travel_____

Name (print)	Document type /Doc. name	Witness Name (print)	Date and Time Notarized _____ ____ _____ am / pm
Phone # / E-mail	Date of document	Witness Phone # / E-mail	Print of Right Thumb
Address	Satisfactory evidence of ID ☐ Driver's license ☐ Known Personally ☐ Credible Witness(es) ☐ Passport ☐ I.D. Card ☐ See Notes	Witness Address	
☐ ID. Issued by ☐ I.D. Number	☐ Expiration Date ☐ Issue Date	Notes	
Signer Signature		Witness Signature	

172
Service: ☐ Acknowledgment ☐ Oath/Affirmation ☐ Jurat ☐ Other/See Notes Fee $_____ Travel_____

Name (print)	Document type /Doc. name	Witness Name (print)	Date and Time Notarized _____ ____ _____ am / pm
Phone # / E-mail	Date of document	Witness Phone # / E-mail	Print of Right Thumb
Address	Satisfactory evidence of ID ☐ Driver's license ☐ Known Personally ☐ Credible Witness(es) ☐ Passport ☐ I.D. Card ☐ See Notes	Witness Address	
☐ ID. Issued by ☐ I.D. Number	☐ Expiration Date ☐ Issue Date	Notes	
Signer Signature		Witness Signature	

NOTARY PUBLIC JOURNAL – LARGE ENTRIES | 89

173 Service: ☐ Acknowledgment ☐ Oath/Affirmation ☐ Jurat ☐ Other/See Notes Fee $_____ Travel_____

Name (print)	Document type /Doc. name	Witness Name (print)	Date and Time Notarized _____ ___ ___ am / pm
Phone # / E-mail	Date of document	Witness Phone # / E-mail	Print of Right Thumb
Address	Satisfactory evidence of ID ☐ Driver's license ☐ Known Personally ☐ Credible Witness(es) ☐ Passport ☐ I.D. Card ☐ See Notes	Witness Address	
☐ ID. Issued by	☐ Expiration Date	Notes	
☐ I.D. Number	☐ Issue Date		
Signer Signature		Witness Signature	

174 Service: ☐ Acknowledgment ☐ Oath/Affirmation ☐ Jurat ☐ Other/See Notes Fee $_____ Travel_____

Name (print)	Document type /Doc. name	Witness Name (print)	Date and Time Notarized _____ ___ ___ am / pm
Phone # / E-mail	Date of document	Witness Phone # / E-mail	Print of Right Thumb
Address	Satisfactory evidence of ID ☐ Driver's license ☐ Known Personally ☐ Credible Witness(es) ☐ Passport ☐ I.D. Card ☐ See Notes	Witness Address	
☐ ID. Issued by	☐ Expiration Date	Notes	
☐ I.D. Number	☐ Issue Date		
Signer Signature		Witness Signature	

NOTARY PUBLIC JOURNAL – LARGE ENTRIES

175
Service: ☐ Acknowledgment ☐ Oath/Affirmation ☐ Jurat ☐ Other/See Notes   Fee $_____   Travel_____

Name (print)	Document type /Doc. name	Witness Name (print)	Date and Time Notarized _____ ___ ___ am / pm
Phone # / E-mail	Date of document	Witness Phone # / E-mail	Print of Right Thumb
Address	Satisfactory evidence of ID ☐ Driver's license ☐ Known Personally ☐ Credible Witness(es) ☐ Passport ☐ I.D. Card ☐ See Notes	Witness Address	
☐ ID. Issued by ☐ I.D. Number	☐ Expiration Date ☐ Issue Date	Notes	
Signer Signature		Witness Signature	

176
Service: ☐ Acknowledgment ☐ Oath/Affirmation ☐ Jurat ☐ Other/See Notes   Fee $_____   Travel_____

Name (print)	Document type /Doc. name	Witness Name (print)	Date and Time Notarized _____ ___ ___ am / pm
Phone # / E-mail	Date of document	Witness Phone # / E-mail	Print of Right Thumb
Address	Satisfactory evidence of ID ☐ Driver's license ☐ Known Personally ☐ Credible Witness(es) ☐ Passport ☐ I.D. Card ☐ See Notes	Witness Address	
☐ ID. Issued by ☐ I.D. Number	☐ Expiration Date ☐ Issue Date	Notes	
Signer Signature		Witness Signature	

NOTARY PUBLIC JOURNAL – LARGE ENTRIES | 91

177
Service: ☐ Acknowledgment ☐ Oath/Affirmation ☐ Jurat ☐ Other/See Notes   Fee $_____   Travel_____

Name (print)	Document type /Doc. name	Witness Name (print)	Date and Time Notarized _____ ____ _____ am / pm
Phone # / E-mail	Date of document	Witness Phone # / E-mail	Print of Right Thumb
Address	Satisfactory evidence of ID ☐ Driver's license ☐ Known Personally ☐ Credible Witness(es) ☐ Passport ☐ I.D. Card ☐ See Notes	Witness Address	
☐ ID. Issued by ☐ I.D. Number	☐ Expiration Date ☐ Issue Date	Notes	
Signer Signature		Witness Signature	

178
Service: ☐ Acknowledgment ☐ Oath/Affirmation ☐ Jurat ☐ Other/See Notes   Fee $_____   Travel_____

Name (print)	Document type /Doc. name	Witness Name (print)	Date and Time Notarized _____ ____ _____ am / pm
Phone # / E-mail	Date of document	Witness Phone # / E-mail	Print of Right Thumb
Address	Satisfactory evidence of ID ☐ Driver's license ☐ Known Personally ☐ Credible Witness(es) ☐ Passport ☐ I.D. Card ☐ See Notes	Witness Address	
☐ ID. Issued by ☐ I.D. Number	☐ Expiration Date ☐ Issue Date	Notes	
Signer Signature		Witness Signature	

NOTARY PUBLIC JOURNAL – LARGE ENTRIES

179
Service: ☐ Acknowledgment ☐ Oath/Affirmation ☐ Jurat ☐ Other/See Notes Fee $_____ Travel_____

Name (print)	Document type /Doc. name	Witness Name (print)	Date and Time Notarized _____ ____ _____ am / pm
Phone # / E-mail	Date of document	Witness Phone # / E-mail	Print of Right Thumb
Address	Satisfactory evidence of ID ☐ Driver's license ☐ Known Personally ☐ Credible Witness(es) ☐ Passport ☐ I.D. Card ☐ See Notes	Witness Address	
☐ ID. Issued by ☐ I.D. Number	☐ Expiration Date ☐ Issue Date	Notes	
Signer Signature		Witness Signature	

180
Service: ☐ Acknowledgment ☐ Oath/Affirmation ☐ Jurat ☐ Other/See Notes Fee $_____ Travel_____

Name (print)	Document type /Doc. name	Witness Name (print)	Date and Time Notarized _____ ____ _____ am / pm
Phone # / E-mail	Date of document	Witness Phone # / E-mail	Print of Right Thumb
Address	Satisfactory evidence of ID ☐ Driver's license ☐ Known Personally ☐ Credible Witness(es) ☐ Passport ☐ I.D. Card ☐ See Notes	Witness Address	
☐ ID. Issued by ☐ I.D. Number	☐ Expiration Date ☐ Issue Date	Notes	
Signer Signature		Witness Signature	

NOTARY PUBLIC JOURNAL – LARGE ENTRIES | 93

181 Service: ☐ Acknowledgment ☐ Oath/Affirmation ☐ Jurat ☐ Other/See Notes   Fee $_____   Travel_____

Name (print)	Document type /Doc. name	Witness Name (print)	Date and Time Notarized
			_____ ___ _____ am / pm
Phone # / E-mail	Date of document	Witness Phone # / E-mail	Print of Right Thumb
Address	Satisfactory evidence of ID ☐ Driver's license ☐ Known Personally ☐ Credible Witness(es) ☐ Passport ☐ I.D. Card ☐ See Notes	Witness Address	
☐ ID. Issued by	☐ Expiration Date	Notes	
☐ I.D. Number	☐ Issue Date		
Signer Signature		Witness Signature	

182 Service: ☐ Acknowledgment ☐ Oath/Affirmation ☐ Jurat ☐ Other/See Notes   Fee $_____   Travel_____

Name (print)	Document type /Doc. name	Witness Name (print)	Date and Time Notarized
			_____ ___ _____ am / pm
Phone # / E-mail	Date of document	Witness Phone # / E-mail	Print of Right Thumb
Address	Satisfactory evidence of ID ☐ Driver's license ☐ Known Personally ☐ Credible Witness(es) ☐ Passport ☐ I.D. Card ☐ See Notes	Witness Address	
☐ ID. Issued by	☐ Expiration Date	Notes	
☐ I.D. Number	☐ Issue Date		
Signer Signature		Witness Signature	

183

Service: ☐ Acknowledgment ☐ Oath/Affirmation ☐ Jurat ☐ Other/See Notes Fee $_____ Travel_____

Name (print)	Document type /Doc. name	Witness Name (print)	Date and Time Notarized _____ ____ _____ am / pm
Phone # / E-mail	Date of document	Witness Phone # / E-mail	Print of Right Thumb
Address	Satisfactory evidence of ID ☐ Driver's license ☐ Known Personally ☐ Credible Witness(es) ☐ Passport ☐ I.D. Card ☐ See Notes	Witness Address	
☐ ID. Issued by ☐ I.D. Number	☐ Expiration Date ☐ Issue Date	Notes	
Signer Signature		Witness Signature	

184

Service: ☐ Acknowledgment ☐ Oath/Affirmation ☐ Jurat ☐ Other/See Notes Fee $_____ Travel_____

Name (print)	Document type /Doc. name	Witness Name (print)	Date and Time Notarized _____ ____ _____ am / pm
Phone # / E-mail	Date of document	Witness Phone # / E-mail	Print of Right Thumb
Address	Satisfactory evidence of ID ☐ Driver's license ☐ Known Personally ☐ Credible Witness(es) ☐ Passport ☐ I.D. Card ☐ See Notes	Witness Address	
☐ ID. Issued by ☐ I.D. Number	☐ Expiration Date ☐ Issue Date	Notes	
Signer Signature		Witness Signature	

185

Service: ☐ Acknowledgment ☐ Oath/Affirmation ☐ Jurat ☐ Other/See Notes   Fee $_____ Travel_____

Name (print)	Document type /Doc. name	Witness Name (print)	Date and Time Notarized _____ ___ _____ am / pm
Phone # / E-mail	Date of document	Witness Phone # / E-mail	Print of Right Thumb
Address	Satisfactory evidence of ID ☐ Driver's license ☐ Known Personally ☐ Credible Witness(es) ☐ Passport ☐ I.D. Card ☐ See Notes	Witness Address	
☐ ID. Issued by ☐ I.D. Number	☐ Expiration Date ☐ Issue Date	Notes	
Signer Signature		Witness Signature	

186

Service: ☐ Acknowledgment ☐ Oath/Affirmation ☐ Jurat ☐ Other/See Notes   Fee $_____ Travel_____

Name (print)	Document type /Doc. name	Witness Name (print)	Date and Time Notarized _____ ___ _____ am / pm
Phone # / E-mail	Date of document	Witness Phone # / E-mail	Print of Right Thumb
Address	Satisfactory evidence of ID ☐ Driver's license ☐ Known Personally ☐ Credible Witness(es) ☐ Passport ☐ I.D. Card ☐ See Notes	Witness Address	
☐ ID. Issued by ☐ I.D. Number	☐ Expiration Date ☐ Issue Date	Notes	
Signer Signature		Witness Signature	

187

Service: ☐ Acknowledgment ☐ Oath/Affirmation ☐ Jurat ☐ Other/See Notes   Fee $_____   Travel_____

Name (print)	Document type /Doc. name	Witness Name (print)	Date and Time Notarized _____ ___ ___ am / pm
Phone # / E-mail	Date of document	Witness Phone # / E-mail	Print of Right Thumb
Address	Satisfactory evidence of ID ☐ Driver's license ☐ Known Personally ☐ Credible Witness(es) ☐ Passport ☐ I.D. Card ☐ See Notes	Witness Address	
☐ ID. Issued by ☐ I.D. Number	☐ Expiration Date ☐ Issue Date	Notes	
Signer Signature		Witness Signature	

188

Service: ☐ Acknowledgment ☐ Oath/Affirmation ☐ Jurat ☐ Other/See Notes   Fee $_____   Travel_____

Name (print)	Document type /Doc. name	Witness Name (print)	Date and Time Notarized _____ ___ ___ am / pm
Phone # / E-mail	Date of document	Witness Phone # / E-mail	Print of Right Thumb
Address	Satisfactory evidence of ID ☐ Driver's license ☐ Known Personally ☐ Credible Witness(es) ☐ Passport ☐ I.D. Card ☐ See Notes	Witness Address	
☐ ID. Issued by ☐ I.D. Number	☐ Expiration Date ☐ Issue Date	Notes	
Signer Signature		Witness Signature	

NOTARY PUBLIC JOURNAL – LARGE ENTRIES | 97

189 | Service: ☐ Acknowledgment ☐ Oath/Affirmation ☐ Jurat ☐ Other/See Notes Fee $_____ Travel_____

Name (print)	Document type /Doc. name	Witness Name (print)	Date and Time Notarized
			_____ ___ _____ am / pm
Phone # / E-mail	Date of document	Witness Phone # / E-mail	Print of Right Thumb
Address	Satisfactory evidence of ID ☐ Driver's license ☐ Known Personally ☐ Credible Witness(es) ☐ Passport ☐ I.D. Card ☐ See Notes	Witness Address	
☐ ID. Issued by ☐ I.D. Number	☐ Expiration Date ☐ Issue Date	Notes	
Signer Signature		Witness Signature	

190 | Service: ☐ Acknowledgment ☐ Oath/Affirmation ☐ Jurat ☐ Other/See Notes Fee $_____ Travel_____

Name (print)	Document type /Doc. name	Witness Name (print)	Date and Time Notarized
			_____ ___ _____ am / pm
Phone # / E-mail	Date of document	Witness Phone # / E-mail	Print of Right Thumb
Address	Satisfactory evidence of ID ☐ Driver's license ☐ Known Personally ☐ Credible Witness(es) ☐ Passport ☐ I.D. Card ☐ See Notes	Witness Address	
☐ ID. Issued by ☐ I.D. Number	☐ Expiration Date ☐ Issue Date	Notes	
Signer Signature		Witness Signature	

191

Service: ☐ Acknowledgment ☐ Oath/Affirmation ☐ Jurat ☐ Other/See Notes Fee $_____ Travel_____

Name (print)	Document type /Doc. name	Witness Name (print)	Date and Time Notarized
			_____ ___ ___ am / pm
Phone # / E-mail	Date of document	Witness Phone # / E-mail	Print of Right Thumb
Address	Satisfactory evidence of ID ☐ Driver's license ☐ Known Personally ☐ Credible Witness(es) ☐ Passport ☐ I.D. Card ☐ See Notes	Witness Address	
☐ ID. Issued by ☐ I.D. Number	☐ Expiration Date ☐ Issue Date	Notes	
Signer Signature		Witness Signature	

192

Service: ☐ Acknowledgment ☐ Oath/Affirmation ☐ Jurat ☐ Other/See Notes Fee $_____ Travel_____

Name (print)	Document type /Doc. name	Witness Name (print)	Date and Time Notarized
			_____ ___ ___ am / pm
Phone # / E-mail	Date of document	Witness Phone # / E-mail	Print of Right Thumb
Address	Satisfactory evidence of ID ☐ Driver's license ☐ Known Personally ☐ Credible Witness(es) ☐ Passport ☐ I.D. Card ☐ See Notes	Witness Address	
☐ ID. Issued by ☐ I.D. Number	☐ Expiration Date ☐ Issue Date	Notes	
Signer Signature		Witness Signature	

NOTARY PUBLIC JOURNAL – LARGE ENTRIES | 99

193 Service: ☐ Acknowledgment ☐ Oath/Affirmation ☐ Jurat ☐ Other/See Notes   Fee $_____   Travel_____

Name (print)	Document type /Doc. name	Witness Name (print)	Date and Time Notarized
			_____ ___ ___ am / pm
Phone # / E-mail	Date of document	Witness Phone # / E-mail	Print of Right Thumb
Address	Satisfactory evidence of ID ☐ Driver's license ☐ Known Personally ☐ Credible Witness(es) ☐ Passport ☐ I.D. Card ☐ See Notes	Witness Address	
☐ ID. Issued by	☐ Expiration Date	Notes	
☐ I.D. Number	☐ Issue Date		
Signer Signature		Witness Signature	

194 Service: ☐ Acknowledgment ☐ Oath/Affirmation ☐ Jurat ☐ Other/See Notes   Fee $_____   Travel_____

Name (print)	Document type /Doc. name	Witness Name (print)	Date and Time Notarized
			_____ ___ ___ am / pm
Phone # / E-mail	Date of document	Witness Phone # / E-mail	Print of Right Thumb
Address	Satisfactory evidence of ID ☐ Driver's license ☐ Known Personally ☐ Credible Witness(es) ☐ Passport ☐ I.D. Card ☐ See Notes	Witness Address	
☐ ID. Issued by	☐ Expiration Date	Notes	
☐ I.D. Number	☐ Issue Date		
Signer Signature		Witness Signature	

195

Service: ☐ Acknowledgment ☐ Oath/Affirmation ☐ Jurat ☐ Other/See Notes Fee $_____ Travel_____			
Name (print)	Document type /Doc. name	Witness Name (print)	Date and Time Notarized _____ ___ ___ am / pm
Phone # / E-mail	Date of document	Witness Phone # / E-mail	Print of Right Thumb
Address	Satisfactory evidence of ID ☐ Driver's license ☐ Known Personally ☐ Credible Witness(es) ☐ Passport ☐ I.D. Card ☐ See Notes	Witness Address	
☐ ID. Issued by	☐ Expiration Date	Notes	
☐ I.D. Number	☐ Issue Date		
Signer Signature		Witness Signature	

196

Service: ☐ Acknowledgment ☐ Oath/Affirmation ☐ Jurat ☐ Other/See Notes Fee $_____ Travel_____			
Name (print)	Document type /Doc. name	Witness Name (print)	Date and Time Notarized _____ ___ ___ am / pm
Phone # / E-mail	Date of document	Witness Phone # / E-mail	Print of Right Thumb
Address	Satisfactory evidence of ID ☐ Driver's license ☐ Known Personally ☐ Credible Witness(es) ☐ Passport ☐ I.D. Card ☐ See Notes	Witness Address	
☐ ID. Issued by	☐ Expiration Date	Notes	
☐ I.D. Number	☐ Issue Date		
Signer Signature		Witness Signature	

197

Service: ☐ Acknowledgment ☐ Oath/Affirmation ☐ Jurat ☐ Other/See Notes Fee $_____ Travel_____

Name (print)	Document type /Doc. name	Witness Name (print)	Date and Time Notarized _____ ___ _____ am / pm
Phone # / E-mail	Date of document	Witness Phone # / E-mail	Print of Right Thumb
Address	Satisfactory evidence of ID ☐ Driver's license ☐ Known Personally ☐ Credible Witness(es) ☐ Passport ☐ I.D. Card ☐ See Notes	Witness Address	
☐ ID. Issued by	☐ Expiration Date	Notes	
☐ I.D. Number	☐ Issue Date		
Signer Signature		Witness Signature	

198

Service: ☐ Acknowledgment ☐ Oath/Affirmation ☐ Jurat ☐ Other/See Notes Fee $_____ Travel_____

Name (print)	Document type /Doc. name	Witness Name (print)	Date and Time Notarized _____ ___ _____ am / pm
Phone # / E-mail	Date of document	Witness Phone # / E-mail	Print of Right Thumb
Address	Satisfactory evidence of ID ☐ Driver's license ☐ Known Personally ☐ Credible Witness(es) ☐ Passport ☐ I.D. Card ☐ See Notes	Witness Address	
☐ ID. Issued by	☐ Expiration Date	Notes	
☐ I.D. Number	☐ Issue Date		
Signer Signature		Witness Signature	

NOTARY PUBLIC JOURNAL – LARGE ENTRIES

199
Service: ☐ Acknowledgment ☐ Oath/Affirmation ☐ Jurat ☐ Other/See Notes   Fee $_____   Travel_____

Name (print)	Document type /Doc. name	Witness Name (print)	Date and Time Notarized _____ ___ _____ am / pm
Phone # / E-mail	Date of document	Witness Phone # / E-mail	Print of Right Thumb
Address	Satisfactory evidence of ID ☐ Driver's license ☐ Known Personally ☐ Credible Witness(es) ☐ Passport ☐ I.D. Card ☐ See Notes	Witness Address	
☐ ID. Issued by	☐ Expiration Date	Notes	
☐ I.D. Number	☐ Issue Date		
Signer Signature		Witness Signature	

200
Service: ☐ Acknowledgment ☐ Oath/Affirmation ☐ Jurat ☐ Other/See Notes   Fee $_____   Travel_____

Name (print)	Document type /Doc. name	Witness Name (print)	Date and Time Notarized _____ ___ _____ am / pm
Phone # / E-mail	Date of document	Witness Phone # / E-mail	Print of Right Thumb
Address	Satisfactory evidence of ID ☐ Driver's license ☐ Known Personally ☐ Credible Witness(es) ☐ Passport ☐ I.D. Card ☐ See Notes	Witness Address	
☐ ID. Issued by	☐ Expiration Date	Notes	
☐ I.D. Number	☐ Issue Date		
Signer Signature		Witness Signature	

NOTARY PUBLIC JOURNAL – LARGE ENTRIES | 103

201 Service: ☐ Acknowledgment ☐ Oath/Affirmation ☐ Jurat ☐ Other/See Notes Fee $_____ Travel_____

Name (print)	Document type /Doc. name	Witness Name (print)	Date and Time Notarized _____ ___ _____ am / pm
Phone # / E-mail	Date of document	Witness Phone # / E-mail	Print of Right Thumb
Address	Satisfactory evidence of ID ☐ Driver's license ☐ Known Personally ☐ Credible Witness(es) ☐ Passport ☐ I.D. Card ☐ See Notes	Witness Address	
☐ ID. Issued by ☐ I.D. Number	☐ Expiration Date ☐ Issue Date	Notes	
Signer Signature		Witness Signature	

202 Service: ☐ Acknowledgment ☐ Oath/Affirmation ☐ Jurat ☐ Other/See Notes Fee $_____ Travel_____

Name (print)	Document type /Doc. name	Witness Name (print)	Date and Time Notarized _____ ___ _____ am / pm
Phone # / E-mail	Date of document	Witness Phone # / E-mail	Print of Right Thumb
Address	Satisfactory evidence of ID ☐ Driver's license ☐ Known Personally ☐ Credible Witness(es) ☐ Passport ☐ I.D. Card ☐ See Notes	Witness Address	
☐ ID. Issued by ☐ I.D. Number	☐ Expiration Date ☐ Issue Date	Notes	
Signer Signature		Witness Signature	

203

Service: ☐ Acknowledgment ☐ Oath/Affirmation ☐ Jurat ☐ Other/See Notes   Fee $_____   Travel_____

Name (print)	Document type /Doc. name	Witness Name (print)	Date and Time Notarized ____ ____ ____ am / pm
Phone # / E-mail	Date of document	Witness Phone # / E-mail	Print of Right Thumb
Address	Satisfactory evidence of ID ☐ Driver's license ☐ Known Personally ☐ Credible Witness(es) ☐ Passport ☐ I.D. Card ☐ See Notes	Witness Address	
☐ ID. Issued by ☐ I.D. Number	☐ Expiration Date ☐ Issue Date	Notes	
Signer Signature		Witness Signature	

204

Service: ☐ Acknowledgment ☐ Oath/Affirmation ☐ Jurat ☐ Other/See Notes   Fee $_____   Travel_____

Name (print)	Document type /Doc. name	Witness Name (print)	Date and Time Notarized ____ ____ ____ am / pm
Phone # / E-mail	Date of document	Witness Phone # / E-mail	Print of Right Thumb
Address	Satisfactory evidence of ID ☐ Driver's license ☐ Known Personally ☐ Credible Witness(es) ☐ Passport ☐ I.D. Card ☐ See Notes	Witness Address	
☐ ID. Issued by ☐ I.D. Number	☐ Expiration Date ☐ Issue Date	Notes	
Signer Signature		Witness Signature	

NOTARY PUBLIC JOURNAL – LARGE ENTRIES

205

Service: ☐ Acknowledgment ☐ Oath/Affirmation ☐ Jurat ☐ Other/See Notes   Fee $_____   Travel_____

Name (print)	Document type /Doc. name	Witness Name (print)	Date and Time Notarized _____ ____ _____ am / pm
Phone # / E-mail	Date of document	Witness Phone # / E-mail	Print of Right Thumb
Address	Satisfactory evidence of ID ☐ Driver's license ☐ Known Personally ☐ Credible Witness(es) ☐ Passport ☐ I.D. Card ☐ See Notes	Witness Address	
☐ ID. Issued by ☐ I.D. Number	☐ Expiration Date ☐ Issue Date	Notes	
Signer Signature		Witness Signature	

206

Service: ☐ Acknowledgment ☐ Oath/Affirmation ☐ Jurat ☐ Other/See Notes   Fee $_____   Travel_____

Name (print)	Document type /Doc. name	Witness Name (print)	Date and Time Notarized _____ ____ _____ am / pm
Phone # / E-mail	Date of document	Witness Phone # / E-mail	Print of Right Thumb
Address	Satisfactory evidence of ID ☐ Driver's license ☐ Known Personally ☐ Credible Witness(es) ☐ Passport ☐ I.D. Card ☐ See Notes	Witness Address	
☐ ID. Issued by ☐ I.D. Number	☐ Expiration Date ☐ Issue Date	Notes	
Signer Signature		Witness Signature	

NOTARY PUBLIC JOURNAL – LARGE ENTRIES

207

Service: ☐ Acknowledgment ☐ Oath/Affirmation ☐ Jurat ☐ Other/See Notes   Fee $_____   Travel_____

Name (print)	Document type /Doc. name	Witness Name (print)	Date and Time Notarized _____ ___ _____ am / pm
Phone # / E-mail	Date of document	Witness Phone # / E-mail	Print of Right Thumb
Address	Satisfactory evidence of ID ☐ Driver's license ☐ Known Personally ☐ Credible Witness(es) ☐ Passport ☐ I.D. Card ☐ See Notes	Witness Address	
☐ ID. Issued by ☐ I.D. Number	☐ Expiration Date ☐ Issue Date	Notes	
Signer Signature		Witness Signature	

208

Service: ☐ Acknowledgment ☐ Oath/Affirmation ☐ Jurat ☐ Other/See Notes   Fee $_____   Travel_____

Name (print)	Document type /Doc. name	Witness Name (print)	Date and Time Notarized _____ ___ _____ am / pm
Phone # / E-mail	Date of document	Witness Phone # / E-mail	Print of Right Thumb
Address	Satisfactory evidence of ID ☐ Driver's license ☐ Known Personally ☐ Credible Witness(es) ☐ Passport ☐ I.D. Card ☐ See Notes	Witness Address	
☐ ID. Issued by ☐ I.D. Number	☐ Expiration Date ☐ Issue Date	Notes	
Signer Signature		Witness Signature	

NOTARY PUBLIC JOURNAL – LARGE ENTRIES | 107

209 Service: ☐ Acknowledgment ☐ Oath/Affirmation ☐ Jurat ☐ Other/See Notes Fee $_____ Travel_____

Name (print)	Document type /Doc. name	Witness Name (print)	Date and Time Notarized _____ ___ ___ am / pm
Phone # / E-mail	Date of document	Witness Phone # / E-mail	Print of Right Thumb
Address	Satisfactory evidence of ID ☐ Driver's license ☐ Known Personally ☐ Credible Witness(es) ☐ Passport ☐ I.D. Card ☐ See Notes	Witness Address	
☐ ID. Issued by ☐ I.D. Number	☐ Expiration Date ☐ Issue Date	Notes	
Signer Signature		Witness Signature	

210 Service: ☐ Acknowledgment ☐ Oath/Affirmation ☐ Jurat ☐ Other/See Notes Fee $_____ Travel_____

Name (print)	Document type /Doc. name	Witness Name (print)	Date and Time Notarized _____ ___ ___ am / pm
Phone # / E-mail	Date of document	Witness Phone # / E-mail	Print of Right Thumb
Address	Satisfactory evidence of ID ☐ Driver's license ☐ Known Personally ☐ Credible Witness(es) ☐ Passport ☐ I.D. Card ☐ See Notes	Witness Address	
☐ ID. Issued by ☐ I.D. Number	☐ Expiration Date ☐ Issue Date	Notes	
Signer Signature		Witness Signature	

211

Service: ☐ Acknowledgment ☐ Oath/Affirmation ☐ Jurat ☐ Other/See Notes Fee $_____ Travel_____

Name (print)	Document type /Doc. name	Witness Name (print)	Date and Time Notarized _____ ___ ___ am / pm
Phone # / E-mail	Date of document	Witness Phone # / E-mail	Print of Right Thumb
Address	Satisfactory evidence of ID ☐ Driver's license ☐ Known Personally ☐ Credible Witness(es) ☐ Passport ☐ I.D. Card ☐ See Notes	Witness Address	
☐ ID. Issued by ☐ I.D. Number	☐ Expiration Date ☐ Issue Date	Notes	
Signer Signature		Witness Signature	

212

Service: ☐ Acknowledgment ☐ Oath/Affirmation ☐ Jurat ☐ Other/See Notes Fee $_____ Travel_____

Name (print)	Document type /Doc. name	Witness Name (print)	Date and Time Notarized _____ ___ ___ am / pm
Phone # / E-mail	Date of document	Witness Phone # / E-mail	Print of Right Thumb
Address	Satisfactory evidence of ID ☐ Driver's license ☐ Known Personally ☐ Credible Witness(es) ☐ Passport ☐ I.D. Card ☐ See Notes	Witness Address	
☐ ID. Issued by ☐ I.D. Number	☐ Expiration Date ☐ Issue Date	Notes	
Signer Signature		Witness Signature	

213

Service: ☐ Acknowledgment ☐ Oath/Affirmation ☐ Jurat ☐ Other/See Notes Fee $_____ Travel_____

Name (print)	Document type /Doc. name	Witness Name (print)	Date and Time Notarized _____-____-_____ am / pm
Phone # / E-mail	Date of document	Witness Phone # / E-mail	Print of Right Thumb
Address	Satisfactory evidence of ID ☐ Driver's license ☐ Known Personally ☐ Credible Witness(es) ☐ Passport ☐ I.D. Card ☐ See Notes	Witness Address	
☐ ID. Issued by ☐ I.D. Number	☐ Expiration Date ☐ Issue Date	Notes	
Signer Signature		Witness Signature	

214

Service: ☐ Acknowledgment ☐ Oath/Affirmation ☐ Jurat ☐ Other/See Notes Fee $_____ Travel_____

Name (print)	Document type /Doc. name	Witness Name (print)	Date and Time Notarized _____-____-_____ am / pm
Phone # / E-mail	Date of document	Witness Phone # / E-mail	Print of Right Thumb
Address	Satisfactory evidence of ID ☐ Driver's license ☐ Known Personally ☐ Credible Witness(es) ☐ Passport ☐ I.D. Card ☐ See Notes	Witness Address	
☐ ID. Issued by ☐ I.D. Number	☐ Expiration Date ☐ Issue Date	Notes	
Signer Signature		Witness Signature	

110 NOTARY PUBLIC JOURNAL – LARGE ENTRIES

215 Service: ☐ Acknowledgment ☐ Oath/Affirmation ☐ Jurat ☐ Other/See Notes Fee $_____ Travel_____

Name (print)	Document type /Doc. name	Witness Name (print)	Date and Time Notarized _____ ___ _____ am / pm
Phone # / E-mail	Date of document	Witness Phone # / E-mail	Print of Right Thumb
Address	Satisfactory evidence of ID ☐ Driver's license ☐ Known Personally ☐ Credible Witness(es) ☐ Passport ☐ I.D. Card ☐ See Notes	Witness Address	
☐ ID. Issued by ☐ I.D. Number	☐ Expiration Date ☐ Issue Date	Notes	
Signer Signature		Witness Signature	

216 Service: ☐ Acknowledgment ☐ Oath/Affirmation ☐ Jurat ☐ Other/See Notes Fee $_____ Travel_____

Name (print)	Document type /Doc. name	Witness Name (print)	Date and Time Notarized _____ ___ _____ am / pm
Phone # / E-mail	Date of document	Witness Phone # / E-mail	Print of Right Thumb
Address	Satisfactory evidence of ID ☐ Driver's license ☐ Known Personally ☐ Credible Witness(es) ☐ Passport ☐ I.D. Card ☐ See Notes	Witness Address	
☐ ID. Issued by ☐ I.D. Number	☐ Expiration Date ☐ Issue Date	Notes	
Signer Signature		Witness Signature	

NOTARY PUBLIC JOURNAL – LARGE ENTRIES | 111

217
Service: ☐ Acknowledgment ☐ Oath/Affirmation ☐ Jurat ☐ Other/See Notes   Fee $_____   Travel _____

Name (print)	Document type /Doc. name	Witness Name (print)	Date and Time Notarized ____ ____ ____ am / pm
Phone # / E-mail	Date of document	Witness Phone # / E-mail	Print of Right Thumb
Address	Satisfactory evidence of ID ☐ Driver's license ☐ Known Personally ☐ Credible Witness(es) ☐ Passport ☐ I.D. Card ☐ See Notes	Witness Address	
☐ ID. Issued by ☐ I.D. Number	☐ Expiration Date ☐ Issue Date	Notes	
Signer Signature		Witness Signature	

218
Service: ☐ Acknowledgment ☐ Oath/Affirmation ☐ Jurat ☐ Other/See Notes   Fee $_____   Travel _____

Name (print)	Document type /Doc. name	Witness Name (print)	Date and Time Notarized ____ ____ ____ am / pm
Phone # / E-mail	Date of document	Witness Phone # / E-mail	Print of Right Thumb
Address	Satisfactory evidence of ID ☐ Driver's license ☐ Known Personally ☐ Credible Witness(es) ☐ Passport ☐ I.D. Card ☐ See Notes	Witness Address	
☐ ID. Issued by ☐ I.D. Number	☐ Expiration Date ☐ Issue Date	Notes	
Signer Signature		Witness Signature	

219

Service: ☐ Acknowledgment ☐ Oath/Affirmation ☐ Jurat ☐ Other/See Notes Fee $_____ Travel_____

Name (print)	Document type /Doc. name	Witness Name (print)	Date and Time Notarized _____ ____ _____ am / pm
Phone # / E-mail	Date of document	Witness Phone # / E-mail	Print of Right Thumb
Address	Satisfactory evidence of ID ☐ Driver's license ☐ Known Personally ☐ Credible Witness(es) ☐ Passport ☐ I.D. Card ☐ See Notes	Witness Address	
☐ ID. Issued by ☐ I.D. Number	☐ Expiration Date ☐ Issue Date	Notes	
Signer Signature		Witness Signature	

220

Service: ☐ Acknowledgment ☐ Oath/Affirmation ☐ Jurat ☐ Other/See Notes Fee $_____ Travel_____

Name (print)	Document type /Doc. name	Witness Name (print)	Date and Time Notarized _____ ____ _____ am / pm
Phone # / E-mail	Date of document	Witness Phone # / E-mail	Print of Right Thumb
Address	Satisfactory evidence of ID ☐ Driver's license ☐ Known Personally ☐ Credible Witness(es) ☐ Passport ☐ I.D. Card ☐ See Notes	Witness Address	
☐ ID. Issued by ☐ I.D. Number	☐ Expiration Date ☐ Issue Date	Notes	
Signer Signature		Witness Signature	

NOTARY PUBLIC JOURNAL – LARGE ENTRIES

221 Service: ☐ Acknowledgment ☐ Oath/Affirmation ☐ Jurat ☐ Other/See Notes Fee $_____ Travel_____

Name (print)	Document type /Doc. name	Witness Name (print)	Date and Time Notarized
			_____ ___ ___ am / pm
Phone # / E-mail	Date of document	Witness Phone # / E-mail	Print of Right Thumb
Address	Satisfactory evidence of ID ☐ Driver's license ☐ Known Personally ☐ Credible Witness(es) ☐ Passport ☐ I.D. Card ☐ See Notes	Witness Address	
☐ ID. Issued by	☐ Expiration Date	Notes	
☐ I.D. Number	☐ Issue Date		
Signer Signature		Witness Signature	

222 Service: ☐ Acknowledgment ☐ Oath/Affirmation ☐ Jurat ☐ Other/See Notes Fee $_____ Travel_____

Name (print)	Document type /Doc. name	Witness Name (print)	Date and Time Notarized
			_____ ___ ___ am / pm
Phone # / E-mail	Date of document	Witness Phone # / E-mail	Print of Right Thumb
Address	Satisfactory evidence of ID ☐ Driver's license ☐ Known Personally ☐ Credible Witness(es) ☐ Passport ☐ I.D. Card ☐ See Notes	Witness Address	
☐ ID. Issued by	☐ Expiration Date	Notes	
☐ I.D. Number	☐ Issue Date		
Signer Signature		Witness Signature	

NOTARY PUBLIC JOURNAL – LARGE ENTRIES

223
Service: ☐ Acknowledgment ☐ Oath/Affirmation ☐ Jurat ☐ Other/See Notes   Fee $_____   Travel_____

Name (print)	Document type /Doc. name	Witness Name (print)	Date and Time Notarized _____ ___ ___ am / pm
Phone # / E-mail	Date of document	Witness Phone # / E-mail	Print of Right Thumb
Address	Satisfactory evidence of ID ☐ Driver's license ☐ Known Personally ☐ Credible Witness(es) ☐ Passport ☐ I.D. Card ☐ See Notes	Witness Address	
☐ ID. Issued by	☐ Expiration Date	Notes	
☐ I.D. Number	☐ Issue Date		
Signer Signature		Witness Signature	

224
Service: ☐ Acknowledgment ☐ Oath/Affirmation ☐ Jurat ☐ Other/See Notes   Fee $_____   Travel_____

Name (print)	Document type /Doc. name	Witness Name (print)	Date and Time Notarized _____ ___ ___ am / pm
Phone # / E-mail	Date of document	Witness Phone # / E-mail	Print of Right Thumb
Address	Satisfactory evidence of ID ☐ Driver's license ☐ Known Personally ☐ Credible Witness(es) ☐ Passport ☐ I.D. Card ☐ See Notes	Witness Address	
☐ ID. Issued by	☐ Expiration Date	Notes	
☐ I.D. Number	☐ Issue Date		
Signer Signature		Witness Signature	

NOTARY PUBLIC JOURNAL – LARGE ENTRIES

225
Service: ☐ Acknowledgment ☐ Oath/Affirmation ☐ Jurat ☐ Other/See Notes Fee $_____ Travel_____

Name (print)	Document type /Doc. name	Witness Name (print)	Date and Time Notarized _____ ___ _____ am / pm
Phone # / E-mail	Date of document	Witness Phone # / E-mail	Print of Right Thumb
Address	Satisfactory evidence of ID ☐ Driver's license ☐ Known Personally ☐ Credible Witness(es) ☐ Passport ☐ I.D. Card ☐ See Notes	Witness Address	
☐ ID. Issued by ☐ I.D. Number	☐ Expiration Date ☐ Issue Date	Notes	
Signer Signature		Witness Signature	

226
Service: ☐ Acknowledgment ☐ Oath/Affirmation ☐ Jurat ☐ Other/See Notes Fee $_____ Travel_____

Name (print)	Document type /Doc. name	Witness Name (print)	Date and Time Notarized _____ ___ _____ am / pm
Phone # / E-mail	Date of document	Witness Phone # / E-mail	Print of Right Thumb
Address	Satisfactory evidence of ID ☐ Driver's license ☐ Known Personally ☐ Credible Witness(es) ☐ Passport ☐ I.D. Card ☐ See Notes	Witness Address	
☐ ID. Issued by ☐ I.D. Number	☐ Expiration Date ☐ Issue Date	Notes	
Signer Signature		Witness Signature	

227

Service: ☐ Acknowledgment ☐ Oath/Affirmation ☐ Jurat ☐ Other/See Notes   Fee $_____   Travel_____

Name (print)	Document type /Doc. name	Witness Name (print)	Date and Time Notarized
			_____ ___ ___ am / pm
Phone # / E-mail	Date of document	Witness Phone # / E-mail	Print of Right Thumb
Address	Satisfactory evidence of ID ☐ Driver's license ☐ Known Personally ☐ Credible Witness(es) ☐ Passport ☐ I.D. Card ☐ See Notes	Witness Address	
☐ ID. Issued by	☐ Expiration Date	Notes	
☐ I.D. Number	☐ Issue Date		
Signer Signature		Witness Signature	

228

Service: ☐ Acknowledgment ☐ Oath/Affirmation ☐ Jurat ☐ Other/See Notes   Fee $_____   Travel_____

Name (print)	Document type /Doc. name	Witness Name (print)	Date and Time Notarized
			_____ ___ ___ am / pm
Phone # / E-mail	Date of document	Witness Phone # / E-mail	Print of Right Thumb
Address	Satisfactory evidence of ID ☐ Driver's license ☐ Known Personally ☐ Credible Witness(es) ☐ Passport ☐ I.D. Card ☐ See Notes	Witness Address	
☐ ID. Issued by	☐ Expiration Date	Notes	
☐ I.D. Number	☐ Issue Date		
Signer Signature		Witness Signature	

NOTARY PUBLIC JOURNAL – LARGE ENTRIES | 117

229 | Service: ☐ Acknowledgment ☐ Oath/Affirmation ☐ Jurat ☐ Other/See Notes Fee $_____ Travel_____

Name (print)	Document type /Doc. name	Witness Name (print)	Date and Time Notarized _____ ___ _____ am / pm
Phone # / E-mail	Date of document	Witness Phone # / E-mail	Print of Right Thumb
Address	Satisfactory evidence of ID ☐ Driver's license ☐ Known Personally ☐ Credible Witness(es) ☐ Passport ☐ I.D. Card ☐ See Notes	Witness Address	
☐ ID. Issued by ☐ I.D. Number	☐ Expiration Date ☐ Issue Date	Notes	
Signer Signature		Witness Signature	

230 | Service: ☐ Acknowledgment ☐ Oath/Affirmation ☐ Jurat ☐ Other/See Notes Fee $_____ Travel_____

Name (print)	Document type /Doc. name	Witness Name (print)	Date and Time Notarized _____ ___ _____ am / pm
Phone # / E-mail	Date of document	Witness Phone # / E-mail	Print of Right Thumb
Address	Satisfactory evidence of ID ☐ Driver's license ☐ Known Personally ☐ Credible Witness(es) ☐ Passport ☐ I.D. Card ☐ See Notes	Witness Address	
☐ ID. Issued by ☐ I.D. Number	☐ Expiration Date ☐ Issue Date	Notes	
Signer Signature		Witness Signature	

NOTARY PUBLIC JOURNAL – LARGE ENTRIES

231
Service: ☐ Acknowledgment ☐ Oath/Affirmation ☐ Jurat ☐ Other/See Notes   Fee $_____   Travel_____

Name (print)	Document type /Doc. name	Witness Name (print)	Date and Time Notarized _____ __ _____ am / pm
Phone # / E-mail	Date of document	Witness Phone # / E-mail	Print of Right Thumb
Address	Satisfactory evidence of ID ☐ Driver's license ☐ Known Personally ☐ Credible Witness(es) ☐ Passport ☐ I.D. Card ☐ See Notes	Witness Address	
☐ ID. Issued by ☐ I.D. Number	☐ Expiration Date ☐ Issue Date	Notes	
Signer Signature		Witness Signature	

232
Service: ☐ Acknowledgment ☐ Oath/Affirmation ☐ Jurat ☐ Other/See Notes   Fee $_____   Travel_____

Name (print)	Document type /Doc. name	Witness Name (print)	Date and Time Notarized _____ __ _____ am / pm
Phone # / E-mail	Date of document	Witness Phone # / E-mail	Print of Right Thumb
Address	Satisfactory evidence of ID ☐ Driver's license ☐ Known Personally ☐ Credible Witness(es) ☐ Passport ☐ I.D. Card ☐ See Notes	Witness Address	
☐ ID. Issued by ☐ I.D. Number	☐ Expiration Date ☐ Issue Date	Notes	
Signer Signature		Witness Signature	

NOTARY PUBLIC JOURNAL – LARGE ENTRIES | 119

233 | Service: ☐ Acknowledgment ☐ Oath/Affirmation ☐ Jurat ☐ Other/See Notes   Fee $_____   Travel_____

Name (print)	Document type /Doc. name	Witness Name (print)	Date and Time Notarized _____ ___ _____ am / pm
Phone # / E-mail	Date of document	Witness Phone # / E-mail	Print of Right Thumb
Address	Satisfactory evidence of ID ☐ Driver's license ☐ Known Personally ☐ Credible Witness(es) ☐ Passport ☐ I.D. Card ☐ See Notes	Witness Address	
☐ ID. Issued by ☐ I.D. Number	☐ Expiration Date ☐ Issue Date	Notes	
Signer Signature		Witness Signature	

234 | Service: ☐ Acknowledgment ☐ Oath/Affirmation ☐ Jurat ☐ Other/See Notes   Fee $_____   Travel_____

Name (print)	Document type /Doc. name	Witness Name (print)	Date and Time Notarized _____ ___ _____ am / pm
Phone # / E-mail	Date of document	Witness Phone # / E-mail	Print of Right Thumb
Address	Satisfactory evidence of ID ☐ Driver's license ☐ Known Personally ☐ Credible Witness(es) ☐ Passport ☐ I.D. Card ☐ See Notes	Witness Address	
☐ ID. Issued by ☐ I.D. Number	☐ Expiration Date ☐ Issue Date	Notes	
Signer Signature		Witness Signature	

NOTARY PUBLIC JOURNAL – LARGE ENTRIES

235
Service: ☐ Acknowledgment ☐ Oath/Affirmation ☐ Jurat ☐ Other/See Notes Fee $_____ Travel_____

Name (print)	Document type /Doc. name	Witness Name (print)	Date and Time Notarized _____ ___ ___ am / pm
Phone # / E-mail	Date of document	Witness Phone # / E-mail	Print of Right Thumb
Address	Satisfactory evidence of ID ☐ Driver's license ☐ Known Personally ☐ Credible Witness(es) ☐ Passport ☐ I.D. Card ☐ See Notes	Witness Address	
☐ ID. Issued by ☐ I.D. Number	☐ Expiration Date ☐ Issue Date	Notes	
Signer Signature		Witness Signature	

236
Service: ☐ Acknowledgment ☐ Oath/Affirmation ☐ Jurat ☐ Other/See Notes Fee $_____ Travel_____

Name (print)	Document type /Doc. name	Witness Name (print)	Date and Time Notarized _____ ___ ___ am / pm
Phone # / E-mail	Date of document	Witness Phone # / E-mail	Print of Right Thumb
Address	Satisfactory evidence of ID ☐ Driver's license ☐ Known Personally ☐ Credible Witness(es) ☐ Passport ☐ I.D. Card ☐ See Notes	Witness Address	
☐ ID. Issued by ☐ I.D. Number	☐ Expiration Date ☐ Issue Date	Notes	
Signer Signature		Witness Signature	

237

Service: ☐ Acknowledgment ☐ Oath/Affirmation ☐ Jurat ☐ Other/See Notes Fee $_____ Travel_____

Name (print)	Document type /Doc. name	Witness Name (print)	Date and Time Notarized _____ ___ _____ am / pm
Phone # / E-mail	Date of document	Witness Phone # / E-mail	Print of Right Thumb
Address	Satisfactory evidence of ID ☐ Driver's license ☐ Known Personally ☐ Credible Witness(es) ☐ Passport ☐ I.D. Card ☐ See Notes	Witness Address	
☐ ID. Issued by ☐ I.D. Number	☐ Expiration Date ☐ Issue Date	Notes	
Signer Signature		Witness Signature	

238

Service: ☐ Acknowledgment ☐ Oath/Affirmation ☐ Jurat ☐ Other/See Notes Fee $_____ Travel_____

Name (print)	Document type /Doc. name	Witness Name (print)	Date and Time Notarized _____ ___ _____ am / pm
Phone # / E-mail	Date of document	Witness Phone # / E-mail	Print of Right Thumb
Address	Satisfactory evidence of ID ☐ Driver's license ☐ Known Personally ☐ Credible Witness(es) ☐ Passport ☐ I.D. Card ☐ See Notes	Witness Address	
☐ ID. Issued by ☐ I.D. Number	☐ Expiration Date ☐ Issue Date	Notes	
Signer Signature		Witness Signature	

239

Service: ☐ Acknowledgment ☐ Oath/Affirmation ☐ Jurat ☐ Other/See Notes   Fee $_____ Travel_____

Name (print)	Document type /Doc. name	Witness Name (print)	Date and Time Notarized _____ ___ _____ am / pm
Phone # / E-mail	Date of document	Witness Phone # / E-mail	Print of Right Thumb
Address	Satisfactory evidence of ID ☐ Driver's license ☐ Known Personally ☐ Credible Witness(es) ☐ Passport ☐ I.D. Card ☐ See Notes	Witness Address	
☐ ID. Issued by ☐ I.D. Number	☐ Expiration Date ☐ Issue Date	Notes	
Signer Signature		Witness Signature	

240

Service: ☐ Acknowledgment ☐ Oath/Affirmation ☐ Jurat ☐ Other/See Notes   Fee $_____ Travel_____

Name (print)	Document type /Doc. name	Witness Name (print)	Date and Time Notarized _____ ___ _____ am / pm
Phone # / E-mail	Date of document	Witness Phone # / E-mail	Print of Right Thumb
Address	Satisfactory evidence of ID ☐ Driver's license ☐ Known Personally ☐ Credible Witness(es) ☐ Passport ☐ I.D. Card ☐ See Notes	Witness Address	
☐ ID. Issued by ☐ I.D. Number	☐ Expiration Date ☐ Issue Date	Notes	
Signer Signature		Witness Signature	

NOTARY PUBLIC JOURNAL – LARGE ENTRIES | 123

241 Service: ☐ Acknowledgment ☐ Oath/Affirmation ☐ Jurat ☐ Other/See Notes Fee $_____ Travel_____

Name (print)	Document type /Doc. name	Witness Name (print)	Date and Time Notarized _____ ___ _____ am / pm
Phone # / E-mail	Date of document	Witness Phone # / E-mail	Print of Right Thumb
Address	Satisfactory evidence of ID ☐ Driver's license ☐ Known Personally ☐ Credible Witness(es) ☐ Passport ☐ I.D. Card ☐ See Notes	Witness Address	
☐ ID. Issued by ☐ I.D. Number	☐ Expiration Date ☐ Issue Date	Notes	
Signer Signature		Witness Signature	

242 Service: ☐ Acknowledgment ☐ Oath/Affirmation ☐ Jurat ☐ Other/See Notes Fee $_____ Travel_____

Name (print)	Document type /Doc. name	Witness Name (print)	Date and Time Notarized _____ ___ _____ am / pm
Phone # / E-mail	Date of document	Witness Phone # / E-mail	Print of Right Thumb
Address	Satisfactory evidence of ID ☐ Driver's license ☐ Known Personally ☐ Credible Witness(es) ☐ Passport ☐ I.D. Card ☐ See Notes	Witness Address	
☐ ID. Issued by ☐ I.D. Number	☐ Expiration Date ☐ Issue Date	Notes	
Signer Signature		Witness Signature	

243

Service: ☐ Acknowledgment ☐ Oath/Affirmation ☐ Jurat ☐ Other/See Notes Fee $_____ Travel_____

Name (print)	Document type /Doc. name	Witness Name (print)	Date and Time Notarized _____ ___ _____ am / pm
Phone # / E-mail	Date of document	Witness Phone # / E-mail	Print of Right Thumb
Address	Satisfactory evidence of ID ☐ Driver's license ☐ Known Personally ☐ Credible Witness(es) ☐ Passport ☐ I.D. Card ☐ See Notes	Witness Address	
☐ ID. Issued by ☐ I.D. Number	☐ Expiration Date ☐ Issue Date	Notes	
Signer Signature		Witness Signature	

244

Service: ☐ Acknowledgment ☐ Oath/Affirmation ☐ Jurat ☐ Other/See Notes Fee $_____ Travel_____

Name (print)	Document type /Doc. name	Witness Name (print)	Date and Time Notarized _____ ___ _____ am / pm
Phone # / E-mail	Date of document	Witness Phone # / E-mail	Print of Right Thumb
Address	Satisfactory evidence of ID ☐ Driver's license ☐ Known Personally ☐ Credible Witness(es) ☐ Passport ☐ I.D. Card ☐ See Notes	Witness Address	
☐ ID. Issued by ☐ I.D. Number	☐ Expiration Date ☐ Issue Date	Notes	
Signer Signature		Witness Signature	

NOTARY PUBLIC JOURNAL – LARGE ENTRIES | 125

245

Service: ☐ Acknowledgment ☐ Oath/Affirmation ☐ Jurat ☐ Other/See Notes Fee $_____ Travel_____

Name (print)	Document type /Doc. name	Witness Name (print)	Date and Time Notarized _____ ____ _____ am / pm
Phone # / E-mail	Date of document	Witness Phone # / E-mail	Print of Right Thumb
Address	Satisfactory evidence of ID ☐ Driver's license ☐ Known Personally ☐ Credible Witness(es) ☐ Passport ☐ I.D. Card ☐ See Notes	Witness Address	
☐ ID. Issued by ☐ I.D. Number	☐ Expiration Date ☐ Issue Date	Notes	
Signer Signature		Witness Signature	

246

Service: ☐ Acknowledgment ☐ Oath/Affirmation ☐ Jurat ☐ Other/See Notes Fee $_____ Travel_____

Name (print)	Document type /Doc. name	Witness Name (print)	Date and Time Notarized _____ ____ _____ am / pm
Phone # / E-mail	Date of document	Witness Phone # / E-mail	Print of Right Thumb
Address	Satisfactory evidence of ID ☐ Driver's license ☐ Known Personally ☐ Credible Witness(es) ☐ Passport ☐ I.D. Card ☐ See Notes	Witness Address	
☐ ID. Issued by ☐ I.D. Number	☐ Expiration Date ☐ Issue Date	Notes	
Signer Signature		Witness Signature	

247

Service: ☐ Acknowledgment ☐ Oath/Affirmation ☐ Jurat ☐ Other/See Notes   Fee $_____   Travel_____

Name (print)	Document type /Doc. name	Witness Name (print)	Date and Time Notarized _____ ____ _____ am / pm
Phone # / E-mail	Date of document	Witness Phone # / E-mail	Print of Right Thumb
Address	Satisfactory evidence of ID ☐ Driver's license ☐ Known Personally ☐ Credible Witness(es) ☐ Passport ☐ I.D. Card ☐ See Notes	Witness Address	
☐ ID. Issued by ☐ I.D. Number	☐ Expiration Date ☐ Issue Date	Notes	
Signer Signature		Witness Signature	

248

Service: ☐ Acknowledgment ☐ Oath/Affirmation ☐ Jurat ☐ Other/See Notes   Fee $_____   Travel_____

Name (print)	Document type /Doc. name	Witness Name (print)	Date and Time Notarized _____ ____ _____ am / pm
Phone # / E-mail	Date of document	Witness Phone # / E-mail	Print of Right Thumb
Address	Satisfactory evidence of ID ☐ Driver's license ☐ Known Personally ☐ Credible Witness(es) ☐ Passport ☐ I.D. Card ☐ See Notes	Witness Address	
☐ ID. Issued by ☐ I.D. Number	☐ Expiration Date ☐ Issue Date	Notes	
Signer Signature		Witness Signature	

NOTARY PUBLIC JOURNAL – LARGE ENTRIES | 127

249 Service: ☐ Acknowledgment ☐ Oath/Affirmation ☐ Jurat ☐ Other/See Notes Fee $_____ Travel_____

Name (print)	Document type /Doc. name	Witness Name (print)	Date and Time Notarized _____ ___ _____ am / pm
Phone # / E-mail	Date of document	Witness Phone # / E-mail	Print of Right Thumb
Address	Satisfactory evidence of ID ☐ Driver's license ☐ Known Personally ☐ Credible Witness(es) ☐ Passport ☐ I.D. Card ☐ See Notes	Witness Address	
☐ ID. Issued by ☐ I.D. Number	☐ Expiration Date ☐ Issue Date	Notes	
Signer Signature		Witness Signature	

250 Service: ☐ Acknowledgment ☐ Oath/Affirmation ☐ Jurat ☐ Other/See Notes Fee $_____ Travel_____

Name (print)	Document type /Doc. name	Witness Name (print)	Date and Time Notarized _____ ___ _____ am / pm
Phone # / E-mail	Date of document	Witness Phone # / E-mail	Print of Right Thumb
Address	Satisfactory evidence of ID ☐ Driver's license ☐ Known Personally ☐ Credible Witness(es) ☐ Passport ☐ I.D. Card ☐ See Notes	Witness Address	
☐ ID. Issued by ☐ I.D. Number	☐ Expiration Date ☐ Issue Date	Notes	
Signer Signature		Witness Signature	

CPSIA information can be obtained
at www.ICGtesting.com
Printed in the USA
BVHW012143160619
551121BV00022B/58/P